MARVEL
COMICS
75
YEARS OF COVER ART

MARVEL COMICS
75 YEARS OF COVER ART

Written by Alan Cowsill
With a Foreword by Adi Granov

CONTENTS

FOREWORD AND INTRODUCTION   6–7

THE GOLDEN AGE
1938–1956

MARVEL COMICS	10–11
MYSTIC COMICS	11
CAPTAIN AMERICA	12–14
ALL WINNERS	14–15
BLACK KNIGHT	15
STRANGE TALES	16
PATSY WALKER	16
MILLIE THE MODEL	17
MISS AMERICA	18
ALL SELECT	18
MARVEL BOY	19
YOUNG MEN	19

THE SILVER AGE
1956–1970

AVENGERS	22–25
CAPTAIN AMERICA	26–27
INCREDIBLE HULK	28–30
TALES OF SUSPENSE	31
AMAZING ADULT FANTASY	32
STRANGE TALES	32
JOURNEY INTO MYSTERY	33
◼ FEATURED ARTIST JACK KIRBY	34–35
FANTASTIC FOUR	36–42
SUB-MARINER	43
SILVER SURFER	44–45
DAREDEVIL	45
NICK FURY, AGENT OF S.H.I.E.L.D.	46–49
AMAZING FANTASY	50
AMAZING SPIDER-MAN	51–59
◼ FEATURED ARTIST STEVE DITKO	54–55
X-MEN	60–65

THE BRONZE AGE
1970–1986

AVENGERS	68–75
◼ FEATURED ARTIST JOHN BUSCEMA	70
◼ FEATURED ARTIST SAL BUSCEMA	71
CAPTAIN MARVEL	76–77
CAPTAIN AMERICA	78–79
DEFENDERS	80
DOCTOR STRANGE	81
INCREDIBLE HULK	82–83
IRON MAN	84–87
BLACK PANTHER	88
ETERNALS	88
DEVIL DINOSAUR	89
THOR	90–93
FANTASTIC FOUR	94–97
◼ FEATURED ARTIST JOHN BYRNE	98–99
MARVEL TWO-IN-ONE	100
SILVER SURFER	101
AMAZING SPIDER-MAN ANNUAL	102
DAREDEVIL	102–105
HOWARD THE DUCK	106–107
LUKE CAGE, HERO FOR HIRE	108
IRON FIST	109
POWER MAN AND IRON FIST	109
TOMB OF DRACULA	110–111
MARVEL SPOTLIGHT	112
ADVENTURE INTO FEAR	113
TALES OF THE ZOMBIE	114

THE MODERN AGE
1986–

DRACULA LIVES	114	AVENGERS	156–161	ANNIHILATION	233
RAMPAGING HULK	115	NEW AVENGERS	162–163	ANNIHILATION: NOVA	233
MARVEL PREVIEW	116	AVENGERS: THE INITIATIVE	164	ANNIHILATION: CONQUEST—STARLORD	234
AMAZING ADVENTURES	117	THE NEW AVENGERS: ILLUMUNATI	164	NOVA	234
MARVEL PRESENTS	117	AVENGERS CLASSIC	165	ANNIHILATION: CONQUEST	235
STRANGE TALES	118	SECRET AVENGERS	166–167	GUARDIANS OF THE GALAXY	236–237
WARLOCK	119	AVENGERS	168	SECRET INVASION	238
▬▬ COVER DEVELOPMENT		UNCANNY AVENGERS	168	MS. MARVEL (SECRET INVASION)	238
NOVA #1	120–121	AVENGERS VS X-MEN	169	THE MIGHTY AVENGERS	
NOVA	122	CAPTAIN AMERICA	170–177	(SECRET INVASION)	239
MS. MARVEL	122	INCREDIBLE HULK	178–188	GUARDIANS OF THE GALAXY	
MACHINE MAN	123	HULK & THING: HARD KNOCKS	191	(SECRET INVASION)	239
AMAZING SPIDER-MAN	124–133	HAWKEYE	192–195	MARVEL ZOMBIES	240–241
▬▬ FEATURED ARTIST		IRON MAN	196–203	DAREDEVIL	242–253
JOHN ROMITA SR.	130–131	SHE-HULK	204–205	MARVEL KNGHTS	249
MARVEL SUPER HEROES SECRET WARS	132–133	THOR	206–207	▬▬ FEATURED ARTIST	
WHAT IF?	134	THOR: AGES OF THUNDER	208	JOHN ROMITA JR.	246–247
MARVEL TEAM-UP	134	LOKI	209	ELEKTRA	254–255
MARVEL FANFARE	135	JOURNEY INTO MYSTERY	209	THUNDERBOLTS	255
THE NEW MUTANTS	136	FANTASTIC FOUR	210–218	GHOST RIDER	256–257
WOLVERINE	137	FF	219	EARTH X	257
GIANT-SIZE X-MEN	138	BLACK PANTHER	220–221	PUNISHER	258–259
X-MEN	139–141	▬▬ COVER DEVELOPMENT		AMAZING SPIDER-MAN	260–285
UNCANNY X-MEN	142–151	BLACK PANTHER # 1	222–223	DEADPOOL	286–287
LONGSHOT	152	INHUMANS	224–225	ROGUE	288
THE NEW MUTANTS	152	MARVELS	226–227	STORM	288
X-MEN ANNUAL	153	NEXTWAVE: AGENTS OF H.A.T.E.	228	X-MEN: PHOENIX—ENDSONG	289
		THE ULTIMATES	229	WOLVERINE	290–297
		THE INFINITY GAUNTLET	230	ORIGIN	297
		CIVIL WAR	231	UNCANNY X-MEN	298–319
		ANNIHILATION PROLOGUE	232		

FOREWORD

My career and my life have been intrinsically linked with Marvel Comics covers for a long time now, and they are such a strong presence in my reality that it's difficult to be objective about it. I grew up in former Yugoslavia, and even in those dark days before the internet, we had access to a lot of Marvel comics, and they had a big impact on my young mind. The energy and power of the images, featuring these fantastically iconic characters, was so exciting—a window into a world of action and wonder, of stylized modern mythology. My first job for Marvel, over a decade ago, was creating a cover for Iron Man, and my life was never quite the same again...

The iconography and styles of Marvel covers have been, and are, such strong elements of pop culture throughout the decades—from the legendary *Amazing Fantasy* issue #15 cover by Jack Kirby, through to the trippy *Nick Fury, Agent of S.H.I.E.L.D.* by Jim Steranko and *Elektra* by Bill Sienkiewicz, to *Marvels* by Alex Ross...and with some wonderful deviations such as *Silver Surfer: Parable* by one of my heroes, Moebius. They have reflected and shaped the trends in comic books and entertainment at large—never more so than today, when some of the biggest Hollywood movies are so closely linked with the visual styles of those iconic images.

The covers have traditionally always served as an advertisement for what is inside, but along the way they developed a parallel life of their own. They started to be framed as standalone posters, collected as pieces of fine art, and came to be seen by artists themselves as their opportunity to push a bit farther and show their best work; the covers became just as iconic as the characters they were depicting.

As the printing technology got more sophisticated, so did the covers. No longer restricted by the process, they started to become elaborate, often fully painted artworks that could take as long to create as whole comic issues used to back in the early days.

This was where my story with Marvel began. I was a semi-successful illustrator on the fringes of the industry, but with a fully formed painted style which attempted to fuse the iconography of comics with the style and rendering of poster illustrators from times before. The Marvel guys recognized something in it and asked me to illustrate a few covers. My second ever cover for them was the one of Iron Man punching the ground...I didn't know it at the time but I had stumbled upon a formula which would take the ol' Shell Head and me on a fantastic journey, starting with the "Extremis" book, written by Warren Ellis, through to the *Iron Man* and the *Avengers* movies, countless covers, toys, statues, and pretty much anything you could think of putting an image onto. Over the years I have illustrated covers featuring just about every Marvel character there is. It's the best job in the world!

The book in your hands is a wonderful collection of the most iconic and memorable covers from Marvel's 75 years of making comics, a journey through history featuring our favorite heroes and villains. I am delighted to have contributed to the world of Marvel covers and proud for my work to stand alongside so many amazing illustrations by incredible artists, past and present. To me the most exciting thing is that some of the best covers are yet to be created. I cannot wait!

Adi Granov

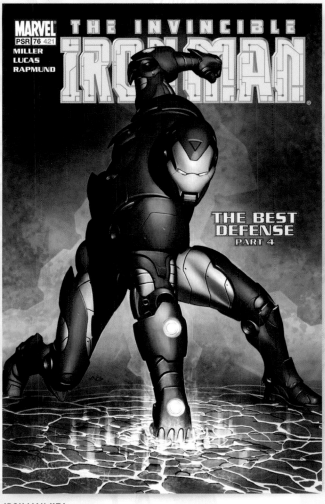

IRON MAN #76
March 2004
Artist: Adi Granov

GUARDIANS OF THE GALAXY #1
May 2013
Artist: Adi Granov

INTRODUCTION

Whether it was Spidey swinging over New York for the first time on Jack Kirby's cover for *Amazing Fantasy* issue #15 or everyone's favorite Avenger appearing on David Aja's *Hawkeye* issue #1, Marvel has always had a knack for creating covers that not only make readers want to read a comic, but *need* to. Indeed, it was the covers that grabbed me as a kid when the *Mighty World of Marvel* was released in the UK way back in 1972.

Selecting the covers for the book...well, that was a daunting task. Some choices were immediately obvious—debuts such as *Fantastic Four* issue #1 could not be omitted! Others were chosen because they best reflect the era they came from, or because they are perfect examples of an artist's style. Of course, opinion on the "best" will always be divided, but we hope that you enjoy delving into this beautiful book and its wide selection of stunning covers.

The book is divided into four chapters, each one covering a comic book era. Within the chapters, covers have been placed in their Marvel "families." So, the Silver Age *Avengers* titles are placed alongside those featuring Avengers characters. At times, this ordering is broken if a theme, story, or artist unites a selection of covers—as it is the art that comes first. And it is the artists that this book is dedicated to. They are the real stars of the show and the ones who have helped make Marvel a household name, creating some of the greatest works of art from the last 75 years along the way.

Alan Cowsill

Alan Cowsill (author)

THE GOLDEN AGE

THE 1930s SAW the new medium of the comic burst into life. Shortly after DC Comics released *Action Comics* issue #1 (June 1938), Marvel Comics—originally known as Timely Comics— unleashed their own Super Heroes into the world in *Marvel Comics* issue #1 (October 1939). The Human Torch and Sub-Mariner were huge hits and soon joined by others such as Captain America and the Destroyer. The stories created during the Golden Age were a clear reflection of the anxiety caused by the Great Depression and the buildup to World War II. Indeed, many of Timely's heroes—such as Captain America— fought the Nazis before America entered the war.

Comic books were a close cousin of pulp magazines such as *Weird Tales* (first published in March 1923). Many artists best known for their work on the pulps, such as Frank R. Paul and Alex Schomburg, brought their eye-catching art styles across to the fledgling comic industry. Young artists such as Jack Kirby and Syd Shores embraced the new art form, creating exciting tales behind colorful, action-packed covers, the likes of which had never been seen before.

ALL WINNERS #4 ▶

Spring 1942
Artist: Al Avison

(Cover shown in full on p14)

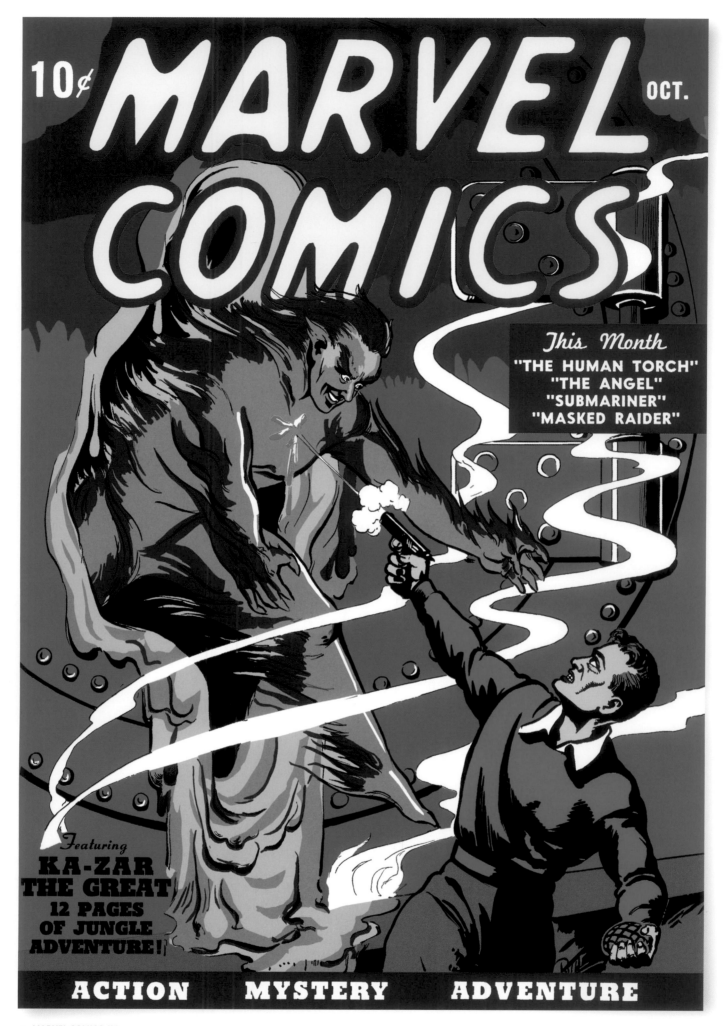

▲ *MARVEL COMICS* #1

October 1939
Artist: Frank R. Paul

Released by Timely Publishing, *Marvel Comics* issue #1
is the most important cover of all time, as it is the one that
launched the company that would become Marvel. Artist
Frank R. Paul remains best known for his work on pulp
magazines. The monstrous look that Paul gave the Human
Torch established the comic as something unique, combining
the then-new Super Hero craze with the look of classic pulps.

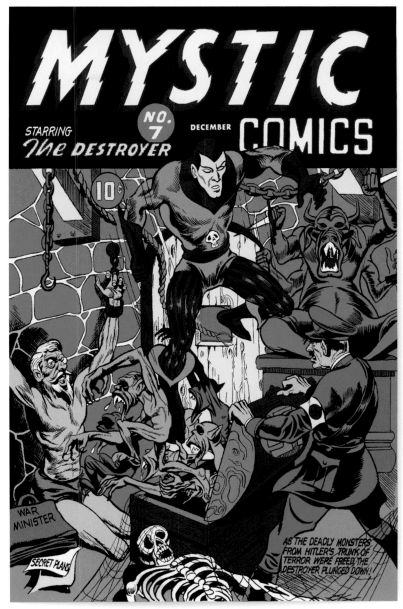

▲ *MARVEL MYSTERY COMICS #15*

January 1941
Artist: Alex Schomburg

Marvel maestro Stan Lee once said,
"Alex Schomburg was to comic books
what Norman Rockwell was to the
Saturday Evening Post." Schomburg excelled
at tension, high-tech machinery, and action—
and this exciting cover to *Marvel Mystery
Comics* shows his style at its best.

▲ *MYSTIC COMICS #7*

December 1941
Artist: Jack Kirby

While the Destroyer has rarely appeared since
the Golden Age, he was one of the most popular
characters of the era, and one of the earliest
co-created by Stan Lee. This dramatic cover, with
its fluid line work and action-packed composition,
is a good example of Kirby's early work.

SMASHING THRU, CAPTAIN AMERICA CAME FACE TO FACE WITH HITLER...

CAPTAIN AMERICA #1

March 1941
Artist: Jack Kirby

Writer Joe Simon and artist Jack Kirby were the greatest team to come out of the Golden Age. They created Captain America for Timely in 1941, the patriotic Super Hero reflecting their own hatred of Hitler before the US entered World War II. The cover to the first issue signalled a clear mission statement: This was a book about heroes opposing the rise of fascism.

▲ *CAPTAIN AMERICA #32*

November 1943
Artist: Syd Shores

Syd Shores started his career inking for Jack Kirby, who was a big influence on his own work. He started pencilling when Kirby briefly joined Timely's competition, and Shores was soon creating fantastic covers of his own. This Cap cover is a great example of Shores' work and also foreshadows Bucky's eventual "death" while trying to stop a drone plane, as recounted in *Avengers* issue #4 *(see p23)*.

▲ *ALL WINNERS #4*

Spring 1942
Artist: Al Avison

This cover reflects the worrying political times more than any other cover of the period, as the heroes march into battle, a burning world below them. Like Syd Shores, Al Avison started as an inker before working as a penciller. The cover also features Whizzer (far left on the cover), the hero Avison helped to create.

▲ *ALL WINNERS #19*

Fall 1946
Artist: Al Avison

The post-war years weren't kind to Super Heroes as other genres proved more popular. Timely tried new ways of grabbing the public's attention though. This classic Al Avison cover showcased the company's most popular heroes as they came together for the very first time to form a supergroup, the All Winners Squad.

▲ *BLACK KNIGHT #1*

May 1955
Artist: Joe Maneely

The cover to the first issue of the *Black Knight* remains one of the gems of the decade. It was illustrated by Joe Maneely, a contemporary of Jack Kirby. Stan Lee declared Maneely would have been an all-time great if he hadn't been tragically killed in a train accident in 1958, at the young age of 32. Maneely was a skilled draughtsman and this cover shows his highly detailed style at its best.

◀ *STRANGE TALES* #1

June 1951
Artist: Carl Burgos

Horror comics were big business in the 1950s, until Fredric Wertham's book *Seduction of the Innocent*, in which he warned about the negative impact of comic books, brought about comic book censorship. Timely produced many horror titles, including the long-running *Strange Tales*. The series' debut issue is a good reflection of their style—weird concepts mixed with bizarre creatures. The cover was illustrated by Carl Burgos, who created the original Human Torch.

◀ *PATSY WALKER* #1

1945
Artist: Mike Sekowsky

Patsy Walker was created by the pioneering female cartoonist Ruth Atkinson, although Mike Sekowsky illustrated the cover to the first issue. A teen humor comic in the same vein as *Millie the Model*, the cover is a good example of Timely's early female characters as the company experimented with various genres. Patsy Walker later became a fully fledged Super Hero when she took on the role of Hellcat in *Avengers* issue #144 (February 1976).

MILLIE THE MODEL #1 ▶

Winter 1945
Artist: Mike Sekowsky

As the Super Hero craze started to wane, Timely tried to find success in other genres. *Millie the Model* proved to be a hit. The cover of the first issue set the style for Millie's romantic, and sometimes slapstick, adventures. The interior artwork was created by Ruth Atkinson.

THE SILVER AGE

THE SILVER AGE saw the birth of Marvel Comics, the company that Timely Publishing eventually evolved into. Due to a decline in the general public's love for Super Heroes in the 1950s, Timely published various comic anthologies dealing with genres as varied as funny animal characters, crime, and horror. The Silver Age started with the publication of DC Comics' *Showcase* issue #4 (October 1956), featuring a new incarnation of The Flash and marking the resurgence of the Super Hero. However, for Marvel fans it really began with *Fantastic Four* issue #1 (November 1961; *see p36*). This was the comic that heralded the launch of the Marvel Universe and a bold new style of storytelling.

This new style—combining fantastical, action-packed adventures with down-to-earth drama—was reflected in many of Marvel's covers. Future artistic legends such as Jack Kirby, Steve Ditko, Gil Kane, and John Romita Sr. created work that tapped into the 1960s zeitgeist, helping to make Marvel Comics the coolest kid on the block. By the end of the Silver Age, Spider-Man, the Hulk, Iron Man, and many other Marvel characters were already on their way to becoming cultural icons.

FANTASTIC FOUR #49 ▶

April 1966
Artist: Jack Kirby
(Cover shown in full on p41)

▲ *AVENGERS* #1

September 1963
Artist: Jack Kirby

By 1963, the Marvel Age of Comics was well underway, with Jack "King" Kirby proving invaluable as he helped build the Marvel Universe. Kirby's cover to the *Avengers*' debut issue brought together Marvel's biggest stars in one, all-powerful super-team. The issue was put together quickly, to replace the late-running *Daredevil* issue #1, but Kirby's artwork made it a smash hit.

▲ *AVENGERS #4*

March 1964
Artist: Jack Kirby

The Silver Age produced many classic covers. As Marvel found new ways of telling stories, they created dramatic covers to go with them—like this masterpiece featuring the return of Captain America. It wasn't the first time Cap's image had been used on a Marvel comic. *Strange Tales* issue #114 featured Cap fighting the Human Torch, but that Cap had proven to be an imposter. This one was very much the real thing.

◄ *AVENGERS* #16

May 1965
Artist: Jack Kirby

If a company had a successful team-book, it was unheard of for them to change the formula. Marvel did just that—with only Cap remaining from the original Avengers line-up. The result is an eye-catching cover focusing on Cap as he brought together a new team. Removing established heroes from the cover and title and replacing them with relative unknowns was a groundbreaking move.

◄ *AVENGERS* #57

October 1968
Artist: John Buscema

John Buscema was a master of form and dynamic poses. The first appearance of the Vision (inked by George Klein) shows just how powerful Buscema could make a simple image. Aided by an eye-catching coloring job, it remains one of the most memorable Avengers' covers and introduced one of the team's greatest heroes.

◄ *AVENGERS* #48

January 1968
Artist: George Tuska

George Tuska was at the helm for the introduction of a new Black Knight. Best known for his work on Iron Man, Tuska was a Marvel mainstay for much of the Silver Age. This Black Knight was the third incarnation of the character and would become a popular member of the Avengers.

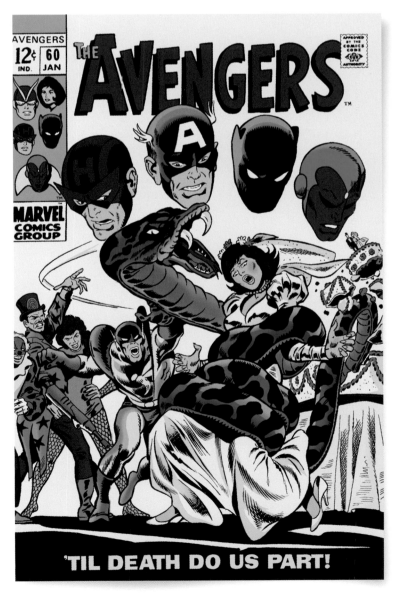

◄ *AVENGERS* #60

January 1969
Artist: John Buscema

Weddings are always stressful—especially for Super Heroes. This John Buscema cover shows the artist at his dynamic best, as the Circus of Crime gatecrashes the Wasp's wedding to Yellowjacket (secretly her long-term beau Henry Pym). It's the sort of mad-but-brilliant concept that made Marvel Comics number one.

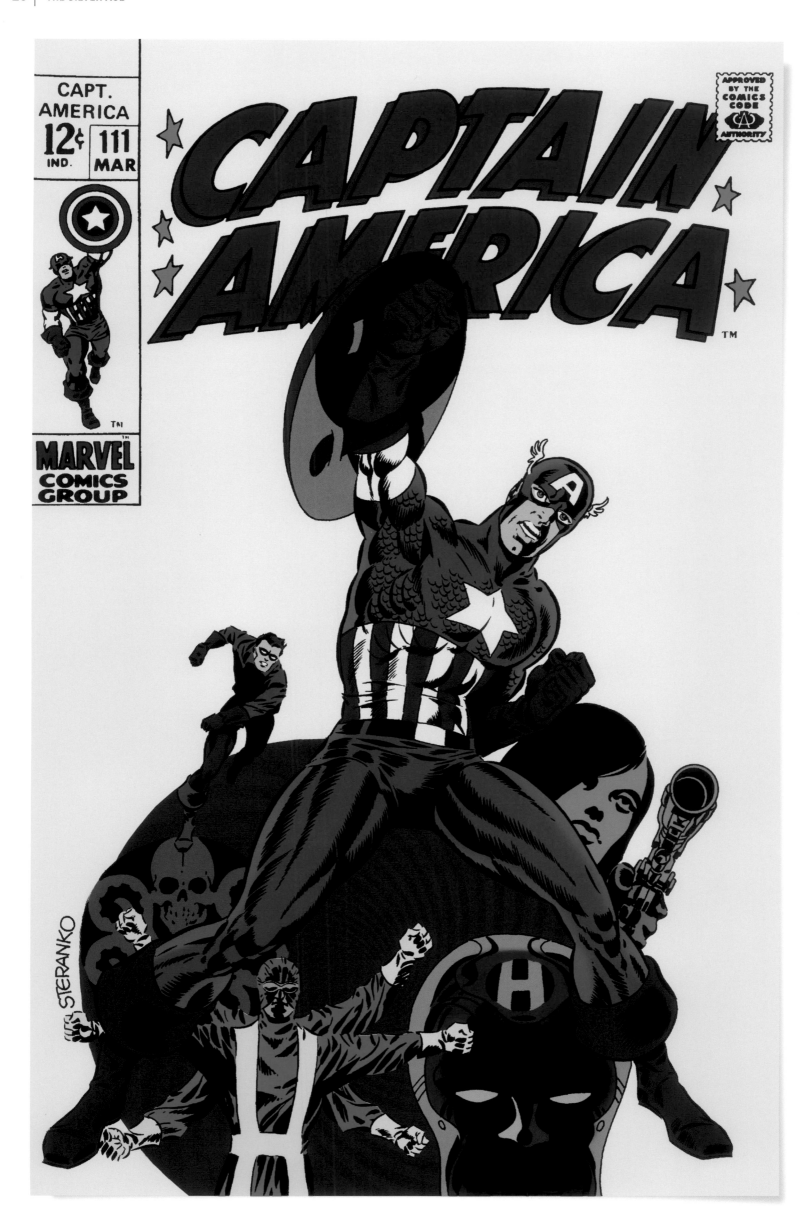

◄ *CAPTAIN AMERICA* #111

March 1969
Artist: Jim Steranko

Few artists have had such an impact as Jim Steranko. He brought a strong design sense to his work that established Marvel's books as cutting edge. This cover is a perfect example of Steranko's skill as a draftsman, while also including some of the more psychedelic elements often seen in his work.

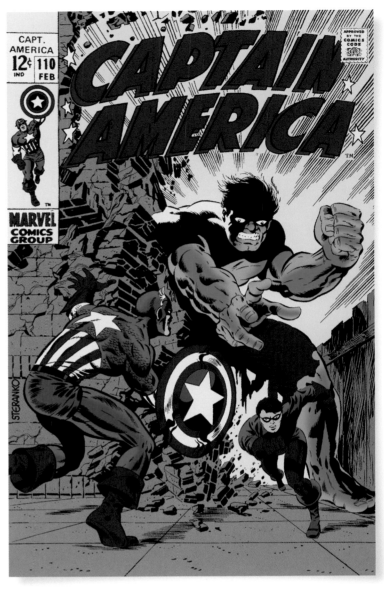

CAPTAIN AMERICA #110 ▶

February 1969
Artist: Jim Steranko

Steranko drew a mean-looking Hulk—as this atmospheric cover shows. The Hulk is all about anger and raw power—facets that Steranko wonderfully brings out in his portrayal of the green-skinned beast. It's a version that also helps make Captain America look all the more heroic.

CAPTAIN AMERICA #113 ▶

May 1969
Artist: Jim Steranko

Another Steranko masterpiece—not that he ever produced anything less. The image of Cap's headstone, with Bucky crying nearby, was sure to grab readers' attention. How can you look at that image and not want to know what was going on inside? That was part of Steranko's brilliance—strong images with even stronger hooks.

◄ *INCREDIBLE HULK* #1

May 1962
Artist: Jack Kirby

Jack Kirby only illustrated the first five issues of *Incredible Hulk*, but his cover to the debut issue firmly established the concept of the Banner-Hulk transformation and created what was to become an iconic image for Marvel. The taglines help pull the reader in, but it is Kirby's powerful central image of Bruce Banner and the Hulk (gray-skinned in his first appearance) that really makes for a dramatic cover.

▲ *INCREDIBLE HULK* #109

November 1968
Artist: Herb Trimpe

Herb Trimpe remains best known for his work on the Hulk, a character he illustrated for seven years in the late 1960s/early 1970s. This early cover (inked by John Severin) shows Marvel's keen eye for design in the way they played with the logo and title to add more impact to the finished cover.

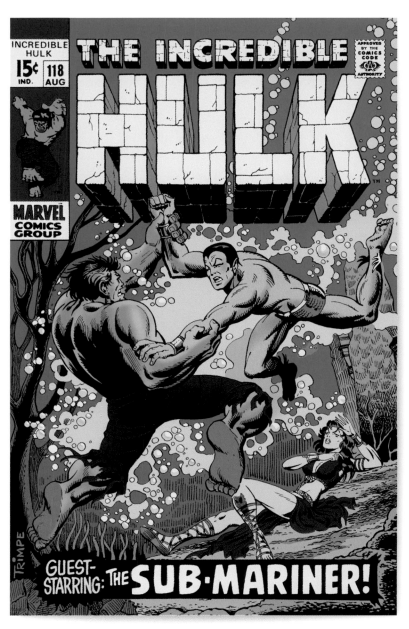

▲ *INCREDIBLE HULK* #118

August 1969
Artist: Herb Trimpe

This early confrontation between the Hulk and Sub-Mariner shows Trimpe at his artistic best. The Sub-Mariner had mostly reformed by this point in Marvel continuity, but a fight between the two heroes was bound to attract the reader—especially as Trimpe manages to convey the power of both characters so well.

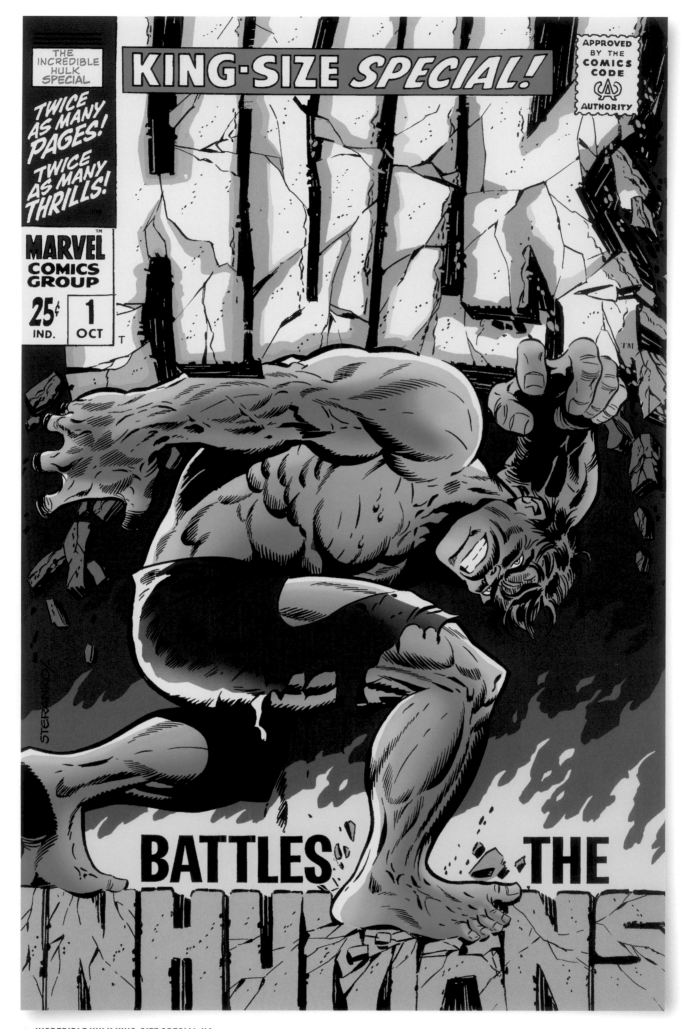

▲ *INCREDIBLE HULK KING-SIZE SPECIAL #1*

October 1968
Artist: Jim Steranko

This cover has proven to be one of the most popular
(and copied) covers of all time. It also harbors a secret—
the Hulk's head isn't by Steranko. The editor wasn't happy
with the original, so he had Marie Severin draw a new
head to paste over the original. It's still regarded as an
epic work—and the full original was later shown in the
UK on *Mighty World of Marvel* issue #129 (March 1979).

▲ *TALES OF SUSPENSE* #39

March 1963
Artist: Jack Kirby

As Marvel's undisputed artistic "King," Jack Kirby was often tasked with creating the covers of key issues, such as the first appearance of Iron Man. The three-panel breakdown next to the large image of Iron Man provided an eye-catching contrast from the regular full-page cover images, and owed a lot to the magazine's past as a horror anthology.

1.

2.

3.

JACK KIRBY

In a career that spanned over seven decades, Kirby is said to have pretty much created the rules of comic book art. This "King of Comics" helped to create many of Marvel's greatest heroes and produced countless legendary covers. With writer Joe Simon, Kirby helped to create Captain America, bringing a sense of humanity to the Super Hero. He worked on a variety of genres, from romance to monster comics, but it is his work for Marvel for which he is best known. The Fantastic Four, Avengers, Thor, Hulk, and the X-Men are just some of the heroes Kirby created with Stan Lee. Their work laid the foundations of the Marvel Universe and brought a new style of storytelling to the medium—one that mixed bombastic cosmic action with down-to-earth drama.

1. *FANTASTIC FOUR #90*

September 1969

This cover (original artwork shown here) is a good example of the mix of the mundane with the alien that made the title such a smash hit. Kirby loved illustrating The Thing—perhaps because Ben Grimm's background was partially based on the artist's own upbringing in Manhattan's Lower Eastside.

2. *FANTASTIC FOUR ANNUAL #3*

October 1965

Jack Kirby worked with Stan Lee to create most of Marvel's heroes and villains—and they all came together for the wedding of Mr. Fantastic and the Invisible Woman in this annual.

3. *THOR #126*

March 1966

Kirby's robust style was perfect for portraying characters of real power—and they didn't come more powerful than Thor and his fellow Asgardian gods. This action-filled cover ripples with energy as Thor and Hercules clash.

4. *FANTASTIC FOUR #72*

March 1968

This cover features two of the elements that Kirby is best known for—the Silver Surfer and the "Kirby Krackle." The latter is an art technique Kirby started to use at this time, using black dots and fractal imagery to denote cosmic energy.

▲ *FANTASTIC FOUR* #3

March 1962
Artist: Jack Kirby

Part of *Fantastic Four*'s success was down to the sheer brilliance of Kirby's artwork and his design of the team and their home. The Fantasti-car is revealed on the cover to issue #3, which also has the FF in costume for the first time. It establishes the book as a unique take on Super Heroes.

▲ *FANTASTIC FOUR* #4

May 1962
Artist: Jack Kirby

The Sub-Mariner made his first Silver Age appearance in this issue. But instead of the hero of old, he was now a villain attempting to destroy the surface world and kidnap Sue Storm. It also proved to be the start of one of Marvel's best love triangles, as Sue Storm found herself torn between the Sub-Mariner and Reed Richards.

◀ *FANTASTIC FOUR* #1

November 1961
Artist: Jack Kirby

The first issue of *Fantastic Four* heralded the start of the Marvel Universe. It also introduced a new type of storytelling—one that mixed soap opera dramatics with amazing stories and fantastical new heroes. Jack Kirby's cover hints at this new direction, as it portrays regular people with amazing powers, fighting a monstrous foe (later revealed as Giganto, a pawn of the Mole Man).

▲ *FANTASTIC FOUR* #9

December 1962
Artist: Jack Kirby

This Kirby creation is pure Hollywood drama as Namor uses his wealth to turn people against the Fantastic Four. The copyline says it all—what happens when the FF can't pay the rent? It was the sort of everyday problem readers could identify with, and it helped make the FF seem more real than many of their contemporaries.

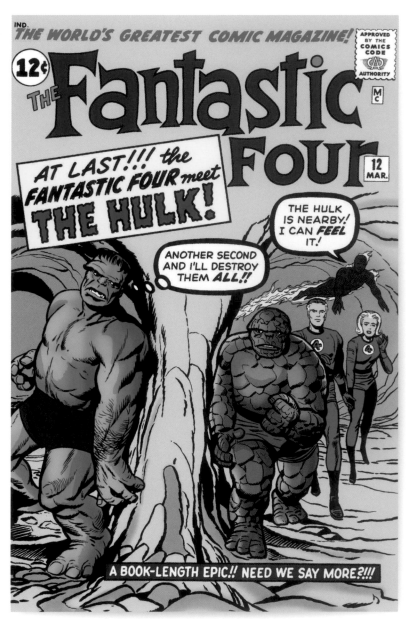

▲ *FANTASTIC FOUR* #12

March 1963
Artist: Jack Kirby

The Thing fighting the Hulk is a slugfest Marvel fans love. The two met for the first time in this issue—the cover teasing the reader with the prospect of their confrontation. Kirby had already started to mutate the Thing into his well-known rocky form, while his Hulk was all about brute force.

▲ *FANTASTIC FOUR* #33

December 1964
Artist: Jack Kirby

Jack Kirby was constantly experimenting with new ways of creating art, sometimes using collages of photos and artwork to create amazing images. These were rarely used on covers, making the cover for *Fantastic Four* issue #33 all the more special. It is a great example of how Kirby constantly pushed the boundaries of comic cover art.

▲ *FANTASTIC FOUR* #46

January 1966
Artist: Jack Kirby

The first few years of the *Fantastic Four* saw Stan Lee and Jack Kirby at their creative peak. Every issue seemed to introduce stunning concepts and bold new heroes. The Inhumans had made their first appearance in the previous issue, but it is their leader, the stunningly designed Black Bolt, who dominates this cover.

▲ *FANTASTIC FOUR #48*

March 1966
Artist: Jack Kirby

Stan Lee and Jack Kirby were about to unleash two of their greatest creations onto the world—Galactus and the Silver Surfer—and they needed a multi-part story to do so. This was one of the first times that the Watcher, a cosmic being who appeared at moments of great importance, was used on a cover to increase the tension. His appearance next to a warning of Galactus communicates a real sense of foreboding.

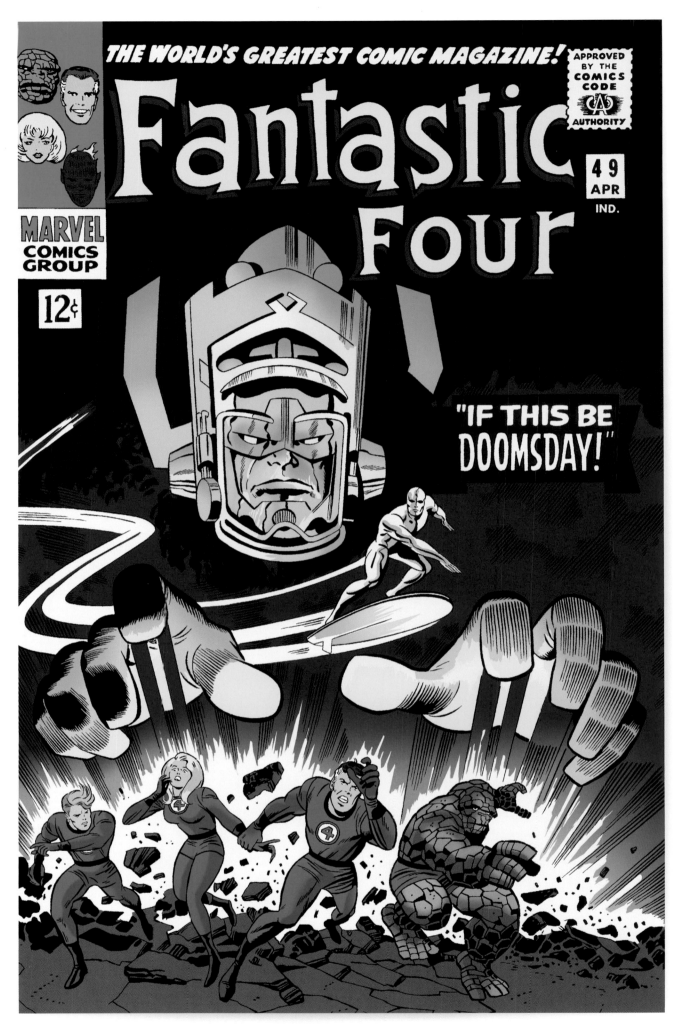

▲ *FANTASTIC FOUR #49*

April 1966
Artist: Jack Kirby

Two of Marvel's greatest characters terrorize the
Fantastic Four on this cover. The planet-devouring Galactus
and his cosmic herald, the Silver Surfer, were the biggest
threat the Fantastic Four had ever faced. The apocalyptic tone
of the cover brilliantly sets up the saga as the FF try to stop
Galactus from destroying Earth. It's an epic that is often
regarded as a high point of the Lee/Kirby era.

◄ FANTASTIC FOUR #51

June 1966
Artist: Jack Kirby

The Thing was the standout character during Kirby's time on the *Fantastic Four*, and he was often front and center on the covers. Kirby's art perfectly evokes the hero's duality as hero and monster. The issue had a shocking twist though—the Thing that his teammates faced wasn't Ben Grimm, but an imposter.

SUB-MARINER #1 ▶

May 1968
Artist: John Buscema

When Prince Namor, the Sub-Mariner, gained a new series, something special was needed for the first cover. Luckily, John Buscema was on hand to illustrate Namor, producing a simple, yet powerful piece. The prince is shown in all his strength and nobility, while a montage in the background shows his history.

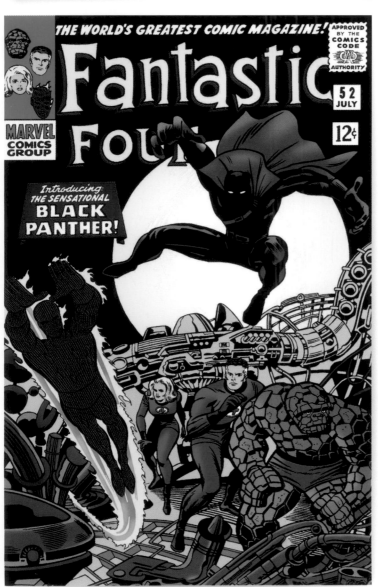

◄ FANTASTIC FOUR #52

July 1966
Artist: Jack Kirby

The 1960s was a period of immense social change—something Marvel's stories often reflected. Stan Lee and Jack Kirby provided another example of their understanding of the zeitgeist with The Black Panther, as they introduced the first mainstream African Super Hero. The cover reflects the story inside, with the Black Panther hunting the FF to test his own skills.

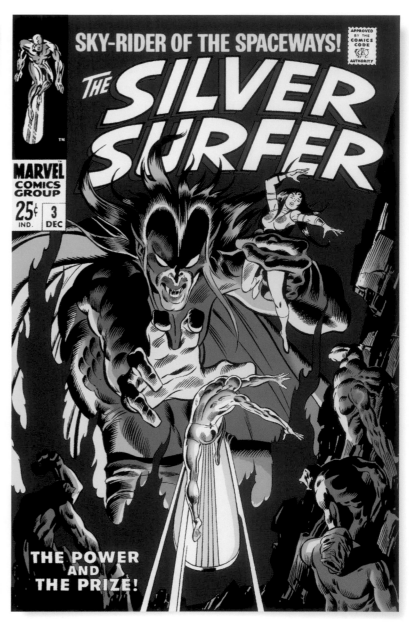

▲ *SILVER SURFER* #1

August 1968
Artist: John Buscema

As soon as the Silver Surfer made his debut in
Fantastic Four issue #48 (March 1966), he became
a fan-favorite. John Buscema brought his art
talents to the regular series, creating a heroic,
but suitably alien Silver Surfer. The cover-line
promises what readers were desperate to learn—
the Silver Surfer's backstory.

▲ *SILVER SURFER* #3

December 1968
Artist: John Buscema

One of the most memorable *Silver Surfer* covers
pits the cosmic hero against Mephisto, Marvel's
answer to the Devil. The evil Mephisto made the
perfect foil for the pure and noble Silver Surfer.
The cover of their first confrontation radiates menace
as the Surfer rushes towards Hell to save his true
love, Shalla Bal. The twisted souls of the damned
framing the scene only add to the sense of danger.

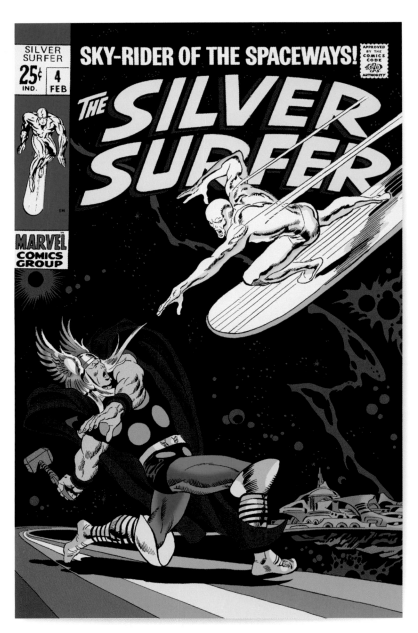

▲ *SILVER SURFER #4*

February 1969
Artist: John Buscema

Buscema was a master of exciting and dynamic cover composition, and this face-off between Thor and the Surfer perfectly radiates the power of the two heroes. It draws the reader's eye into the heart of the action, and leaves them really needing to know what would happen when the two titans clashed.

▲ *DAREDEVIL #1*

April 1964
Artists: Jack Kirby and Bill Everett

Bill Everett was the main artist on *Daredevil*'s debut issue, but when he fell behind schedule, Jack Kirby was called in to help out. The cover and issue included work by both of them, and Steve Ditko and inker Sol Bodsky also contributed. The cover uses elements of Marvel's old romance comics and makes the most of Spider-Man and the Fantastic Four's success to help sell the new hero.

NICK FURY, AGENT OF S.H.I.E.L.D. #4

September 1968
Artist: Jim Steranko

Jim Steranko started working for Marvel in 1966 on Nick Fury's adventures in *Strange Tales* issue #151 (December 1966). It was after Fury gained his own title, however, that Steranko produced the Marvel work he is best known for. The cover to issue #4 reflects Steranko's embrace of outside influences on his work—in this case, Op Art, as seen in the dazzling black and white background.

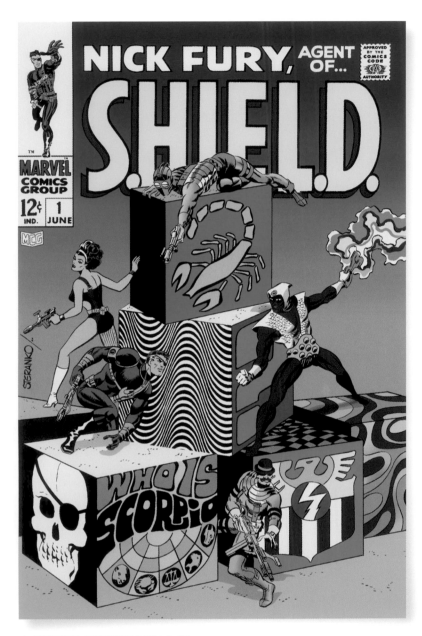

▲ *NICK FURY, AGENT OF S.H.I.E.L.D. #1*

June 1968
Artist: Jim Steranko

When Jim Steranko was given a full comic to illustrate, he created one of the most-revered series in the medium. The cover to the first issue saw Steranko use text as part the main image—creating a new element of cover design in the process and producing a cover the like of which had never been seen before at Marvel.

▲ *NICK FURY, AGENT OF S.H.I.E.L.D. #3*

August 1968
Artist: Jim Steranko

This Steranko cover highlights his skill as a colorist as well as an artist. With echoes of the classic novel *Hound of the Baskervilles*, the story had Nick Fury traveling to Scotland to help an old war colleague. Steranko's use of moody colors complements his pencils to give the cover a dark and sinister atmosphere.

▲ *NICK FURY, AGENT OF S.H.I.E.L.D.* #6

November 1968
Artist: Jim Steranko

Although Steranko stopped handling the interior artwork with this issue, he did create one of his best covers. This striking image of Nick Fury in space, with the moon looming behind him, was produced at the height of the Space Race. With the Earth exploding in the distance, it's the kind of high-impact, beautifully drawn cover that Steranko excelled at.

▲ *NICK FURY, AGENT OF S.H.I.E.L.D.* #7

December 1968
Artist: Jim Steranko

Jim Steranko's last cover for the title (except for the collections) owes something to the work of Salvador Dali, with its melting landscape and nightmarish figures. Steranko eventually returned to the more lucrative world of advertising, but his comic art remains some of the best to have ever graced the medium.

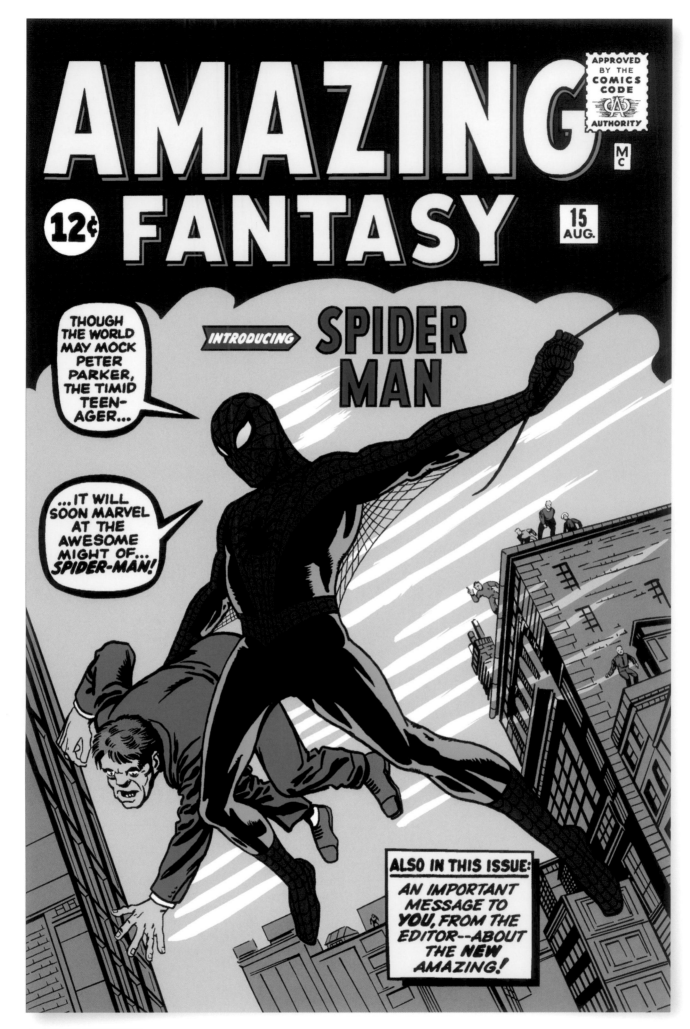

▲ *AMAZING FANTASY #15*

August 1962
Artist: Jack Kirby

While Steve Ditko illustrated Spider-Man's first appearance,
Marvel boss Stan Lee didn't think his original cover was
heroic enough and got Jack Kirby to provide a fresh take.
Kirby's image is arguably the most famous in Marvel's history
and shows the creators at their game-changing best. At the time,
the consensus was that teenage heroes couldn't be the main
character. Spidey's success changed that idea forever.

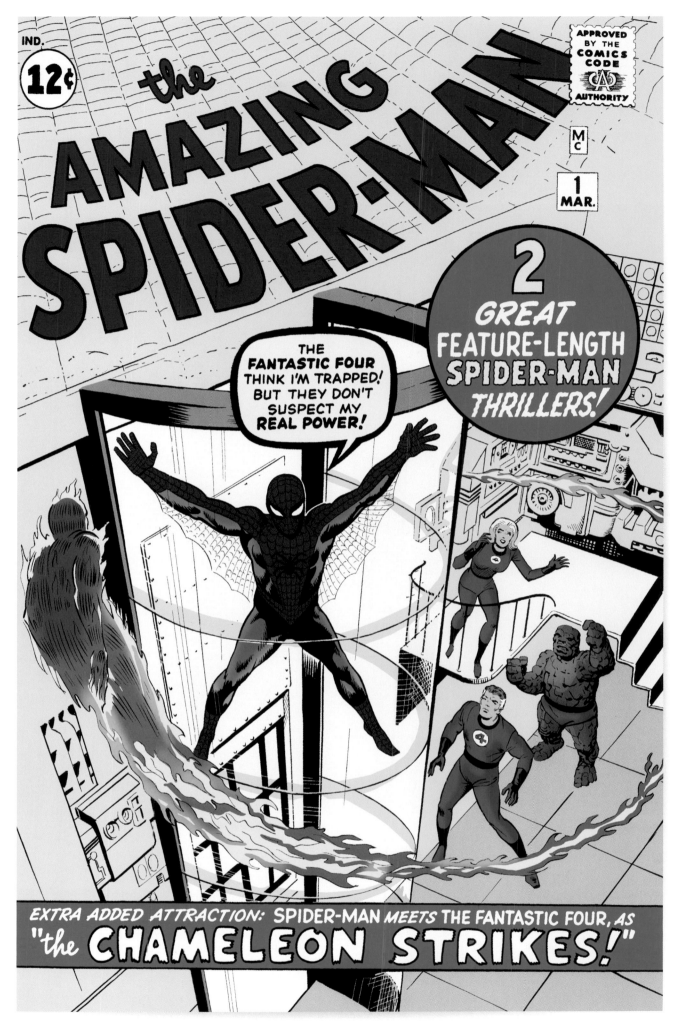

▲ *AMAZING SPIDER-MAN* #1

March 1963
Artists: Jack Kirby and Steve Ditko

Jack Kirby and Steve Ditko joined forces for the cover of
Amazing Spider-Man issue #1, with Ditko inking Kirby's heroic-
looking pencils. The image of Spidey meeting the Fantastic Four
was commercially a strong one. The FF had proven to be a big hit
and having them on the cover would help attract readers to the
new book. It was also a sign of the interconnected universe that
would help make Marvel so popular.

1.

2.

3.

STEVE DITKO

Alongside Jack Kirby and John Romita Sr., Steve Ditko was a key artist in Marvel's history, co-creating two of their greatest characters—Doctor Strange and Spider-Man. His work had a realistic noir-like quality to it—whether he was illustrating a cover or designing strange-looking characters such as the Green Goblin. Lee got Ditko on board to work on Spidey, believing Ditko's more naturalistic style would suit the teenage Super Hero better than Kirby's larger-than-life work. Ditko also brought Doctor Strange to life, creating surreal and nightmarish worlds and fantastically weird creatures. Despite quitting *Amazing Spider-Man* after only 38 issues and leaving Marvel, this visionary man's work influenced countless artists who followed.

1. *AMAZING FANTASY* #15

August 1962

Although Steve Ditko helped to create Spider-Man, this original cover for the webslinger's first appearance was never used. Instead, Jack Kirby drew a more heroic version *(see p50)*. Ditko's original art exemplifies his more realistic approach.

2. *AMAZING ADULT FANTASY* #12

May 1962

Ditko's artistic style found a home in *Amazing Adult Fantasy*, a short-lived anthology that showcased his realistic but sometimes nightmarish work. This cover highlights Ditko's skill at mixing the everyday with the bizarre.

3. *STRANGE TALES* #146

July 1966

Ditko's inventive art style came into its own depicting the adventures of Doctor Strange. This cover shows Doctor Strange facing another surreal Lee/Ditko creation— Eternity, a being made up of the fabric of existence.

4. *AMAZING SPIDER-MAN ANNUAL* #1

October 1964

During his run on *Amazing Spider-Man*, Ditko co-created many of the webslinger's greatest foes, including Doctor Octopus and the Lizard. The first *Amazing Spider-Man Annual* bought six of them together in one sinister team.

AMAZING SPIDER-MAN #39 ▶

August 1966
Artist: John Romita Sr.

Following the success of Steve Ditko was a tough task, but John Romita Sr. was an inspired choice. At the time, Romita was best known for his work on romance comics, but he brought a more hip style to Spider-Man. His first cover promises readers a long-awaited revelation: Who was behind the Green Goblin's mask?

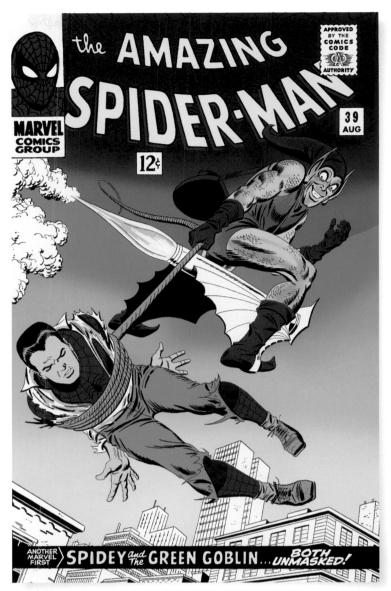

AMAZING SPIDER-MAN #40 ▶

September 1966
Artist: John Romita Sr.

A companion piece to Romita's first *Amazing Spider-Man* cover, this issue saw a rage-filled Spidey taking on the Green Goblin. With Steve Ditko gone, writer Stan Lee knew he needed something special to pull the readers in. These two covers did just that. Romita's dynamic, modern style soon made Spider-Man more popular than ever.

◀ *AMAZING SPIDER-MAN #33*

February 1966
Artist: Steve Ditko

This issue is often voted one of the best Spider-Man comics of all time. It might appear to be a simple cover, but the image of Spidey trapped under the machinery encapsulates many of Lee and Ditko's stories, in which the webslinger tries to beat overwhelming odds. The issue was one of Ditko's last, the artist leaving the title with issue #38.

◀ *X-MEN #50*

November 1968
Artist: Jim Steranko

Steranko briefly created brilliant work
for *X-Men* in the late 1960s. Lorna Dane
(aka Polaris) was the focus in this issue.
Steranko's figure work and the eye-catching
color makes this cover stand out. The
energy in the backdrop also adds to the
sense of power emanating from Lorna.

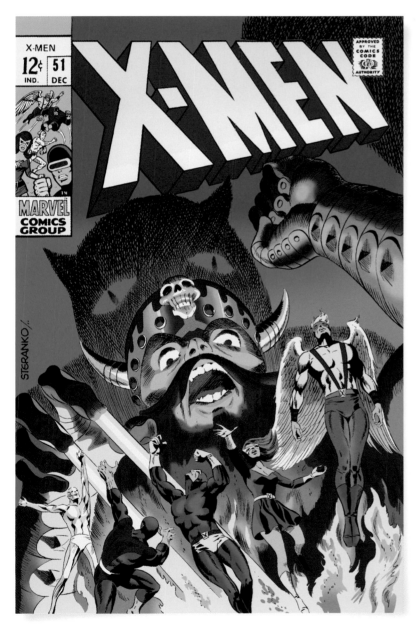

▲ *X-MEN #51*

December 1968
Artist: Jim Steranko

Steranko's short run on *X-Men* ended with this
slightly crazy cover. The image is all about light and
shadow as the X-Men learned the truth about Erik
the Red, and met their old foe Magneto once again.
These later issues took on a more experimental
direction as Marvel tried various ways to boost sales.

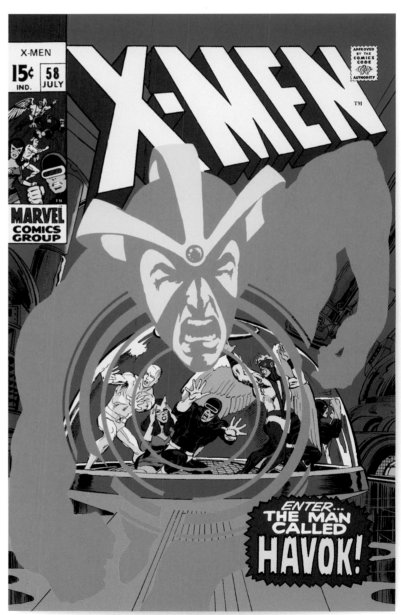

▲ *X-MEN #58*

July 1969
Artist: Neal Adams

Alongside Jim Steranko, Neal Adams helped redefine
what comics could be in the late 1960s. Adams brought
an energy and dynamic layout to his work that continues
to influence artists even today. The cover for this issue
shows Alex Summers as Havok for the first time.
Its inspired layout and color make it ahead of its time.

▲ *X-MEN* #59

August 1969
Artist: Neal Adams

This cover showing Cyclops surrounded by the mutant-hunting Sentinels is a brilliant example of the energy Adams puts into his work. The composition of the piece, with Cyclops in the foreground attempting to hold off his attackers, puts the viewer in the position of Cyclops, encouraging a greater empathy.

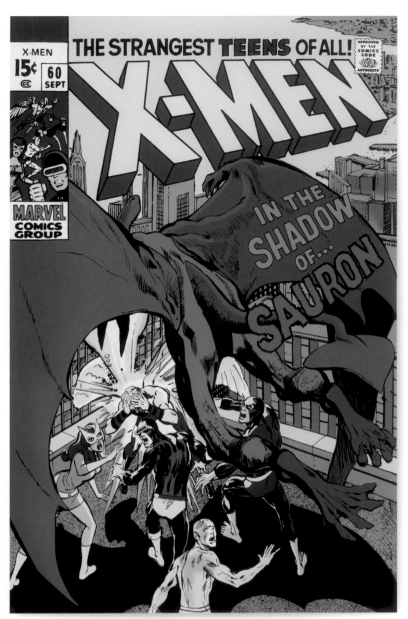

▲ *X-MEN* #60

September 1969
Artist: Neal Adams

This memorable cover by Adams introduced Sauron, one of the X-Men's strangest-looking foes. The flow and energy for which Adams' art is renowned is once again present. This issue took the X-Men to the Savage Land in a classic four-part tale.

X-MEN #62 ▶

November 1969
Artist: Neal Adams

One of Neal Adams' final covers on the *X-Men* was another classic, this time featuring Ka-Zar, Lord of the Savage Land, and his loyal Sabertooth tiger Zabu. The text carved into the rock echoes one of Ka-Zar's previous cover appearances on *The Incredible Hulk* issue #109 *(see p29)*.

THE BRONZE AGE

THE BRONZE AGE was a period of amazing change. A whole host of talented new artists and writers began to make their mark on the industry, and comics started to take on a more realistic approach. For Marvel, it began with *Amazing Spider-Man* issue #96 (May 1971), when they published a storyline dealing with Harry Osborn's drug addiction—without the approval of the Comics Code Authority (which acted as a censor.) This led to an updating of the code, which in turn allowed horror comics to make a comeback and for others to include more adult themes.

Artists such as Neal Adams and Jim Steranko pushed cover design in bold new directions. They were soon joined by future art legends George Pérez, John Byrne, and Frank Miller. It was also a time when comic collecting became very popular, and the increased number of comic shops meant that Marvel could start selling their books straight to specialist shops. By the end of the Bronze Age, the industry had almost changed beyond recognition.

MARVEL SUPER HEROES
SECRET WARS #8 ▶

December 1984
Artist: Mike Zeck

(Cover shown in full on p133)

AMID THE CHAOS,

◀ *AVENGERS #83*

December 1970
Artist: John Buscema

By 1970, second-wave feminism was at its peak in the US, so Marvel waded into the political waters by bringing Medusa, Scarlet Witch, Black Widow, and the Wasp together in one story. Valkyrie, a new character despite being Enchantress in disguise, stands front-and-center in this John Buscema image, having finished off the "male chauvinist pigs!"

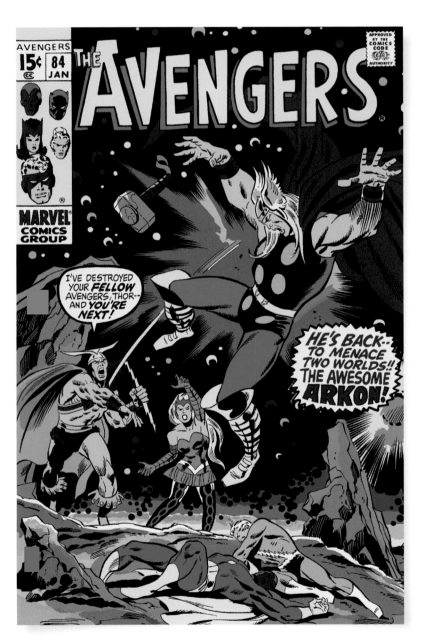

▲ *AVENGERS #84*

January 1971
Artist: John Buscema

Arkon returned to plague the Avengers in this issue. Half hero, half barbarian, Arkon was just the sort of character Buscema excelled at, his style of drawing highly muscular figures bringing a real savagery to the characters. It was a technique Buscema would later bring to his work on *Conan the Barbarian*.

▲ *AVENGERS #87*

April 1971
Artist: John Buscema

Dominated by the powerful figure of the Black Panther, this cover was a key issue in the life of the Super Hero's alter ego, Prince T'Challa. Already a popular character from his appearances in both this title and the *Fantastic Four*, the prospect of finally learning the truth about his origins, combined with the striking cover art, enticed readers.

2.

3.

JOHN BUSCEMA

Alongside Jack Kirby and John Romita Sr., John Buscema was one of Marvel's artistic founding fathers—his storytelling ability and powerful but naturalistic style influencing many of the artists who followed him. For many, he *was* Marvel, even illustrating the book *How to Draw Comics the Marvel Way*. During his long career, John illustrated just about every Marvel character and numerous covers. Some of his best-known work includes the *Avengers* and *Silver Surfer*. However, it is his decade-spanning run on *Conan the Barbarian* that best showcased his exceptional ability to draw powerful physical forms and savage action scenes. It was a facet of his artistic ability that led to John Buscema's nickname—"the Michelangelo of comics."

1. *FANTASTIC FOUR* #109

April 1971

John Buscema was a master of composition, as this piece of original art (inked by Joe Sinnott) shows. It also reflects his skill in conveying movement and action. The signatures include those of editorial as they signed off the work.

2. *FANTASTIC FOUR* #111

June 1971

Together with his exceptional figure work, John is perhaps best known for his ability to portray the raw power of muscular heroes. This dynamic cover is a good example of his style, showing the Thing clashing with his teammate the Human Torch.

3. *AVENGERS* #54

July 1968

John's vibrant and powerful art was a perfect match for the Avengers. The cover to this issue not only highlights the power he was able to instill into his characters, but also his ability to design a dramatic layout.

1.

2.

3.

SAL BUSCEMA

John Buscema's brother Sal originally wanted to be an inker rather than a penciller, but he quickly became one of Marvel's most prolific artists. He pencilled many of their best-selling titles and created a number of striking covers. Sal illustrated all of Marvel's most famous heroes and villains during his long career and enjoyed critically acclaimed runs on the *Avengers*, *Hulk*, and *Captain America*. He is best known for his 10-year run on *Spectacular Spider-Man*, during which he illustrated some of the webslinger's greatest epics, including the "Clone Saga." Sal's loose, energetic style coupled with his fast-paced storytelling (hailed by many as the best in the business) was perfectly suited to illustrating Spidey's action-packed adventures.

1. *SUB-MARINER* #33

January 1971

This Sal Buscema cover (original cover art shown here) is full of tension. Sal artfully conveyed the anger and regret felt by the Sub-Mariner on learning of a huge disaster that had struck Atlantis during his absence from his undersea kingdom.

2. *AVENGERS* #71

December 1969

This energetic fight scene showing the Avengers fighting the Invaders in World War II is a perfect example of Sal's smooth but action-packed style. Sal could put a real sense of movement and drama into his covers.

3. *PETER PARKER, THE SPECTACULAR SPIDER-MAN* #1

December 1976

Sal was the original artist on *The Spectacular Spider-Man* and illustrated over 100 issues of the title. The cover to the first issue is a dramatic one, showing the evil Tarantula mid-air during an attack on Spidey. It is a fine example of Sal's ability to illustrate movement and fast-paced action.

▲ *AVENGERS* #89

June 1971
Artist: Sal Buscema

John Buscema's kid brother, Sal, finally hit the big time in his own right with this stunning work, and he aimed to shock. This cover also marked the start of the Kree/Skrull war storyline. It was not only one of the first multipart epics to feature in the *Avengers*, but was also widely regarded as one of the most exciting and compelling story arcs of its time.

▲ *AVENGERS* #92

September 1971
Artist: Neal Adams

The Kree/Skrull war continued with a twist as the Avengers turned on their own team members. Neal Adam's image of Captain America, Thor, and Iron Man disbanding the team makes a striking cover. However, fans didn't need to mourn for long— all was not as it seemed, and the three Avengers were later revealed to be shape-changing Skrulls.

AVENGERS #118 ▶

December 1973
Artist: Unknown & John Romita Sr.

The Avengers/Defenders war was the first major crossover between the two teams, and John Romita Sr. produced an action-packed scene for the conclusion. It was rare to show this many heroes on a cover, which made its impact even more dramatic. The cover shows the architects of the war—the evil Loki and the dread Dormammu—on the verge of defeating both teams, using the powerful Evil Eye.

◄ AVENGERS #201 ►

November 1980
Artist: George Pérez

Marvel has always had fun with their heroes—it's one of the company's main selling points. This Pérez cover proved the perfect foil for the series of hard-hitting storylines that had preceded it. The image of Jarvis, the Avengers' long-suffering butler, taking control provided a welcome shot of humor to the book: Thor might have wielded a mystical hammer, but Jarvis had a vacuum cleaner!

◄ AVENGERS #160

June 1977
Artist: George Pérez

George Pérez quickly became one of Marvel's leading artists after joining them in the 1970s, and he has been an undisputed star of the comic world ever since. Pérez had a long history with *Avengers* (issue #141 was his first) and produced countless covers regarded as modern-day classics by fans and critics alike— including this early example, showing the Grim Reaper looming over Wonder Man and the Vision.

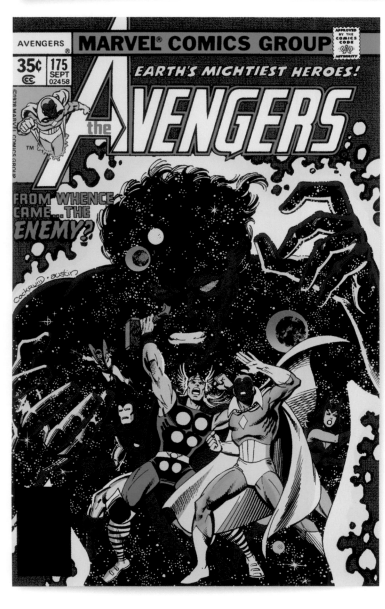

◄ AVENGERS #175

September 1978
Artist: Dave Cockrum

The "Kovac" Saga is regarded as an all-time great, and this dramatic cover by Dave Cockrum encapsulated the cosmic story perfectly. The time-traveling Kovac came from the future, gained God-like abilities, and became one with the universe. He had the power to destroy not only the Avengers, but also the whole world.

▲ *CAPTAIN MARVEL* #28

September 1973
Artist: Jim Starlin

With the Avengers defeated, Jim Starlin's cover presented Captain Marvel as the only hero left to stop the evil Titan Thanos' plans. Thanos appeared on a cover for the first time with this issue and would go on to be one of the greatest villains in the Marvel Universe, even appearing in the post-credits epilogue of *The Avengers* movie of 2012.

▲ *CAPTAIN MARVEL* #29

November 1973
Artist: Jim Starlin

Jim Starlin built his reputation as a writer and artist on *Captain Marvel* before going on to be one of the best-known artists in the business. Starlin was renowned for his intergalactic stories, and this early *Captain Marvel* cover epitomizes his style—a powerful central figure in a rather brilliant cosmic setting.

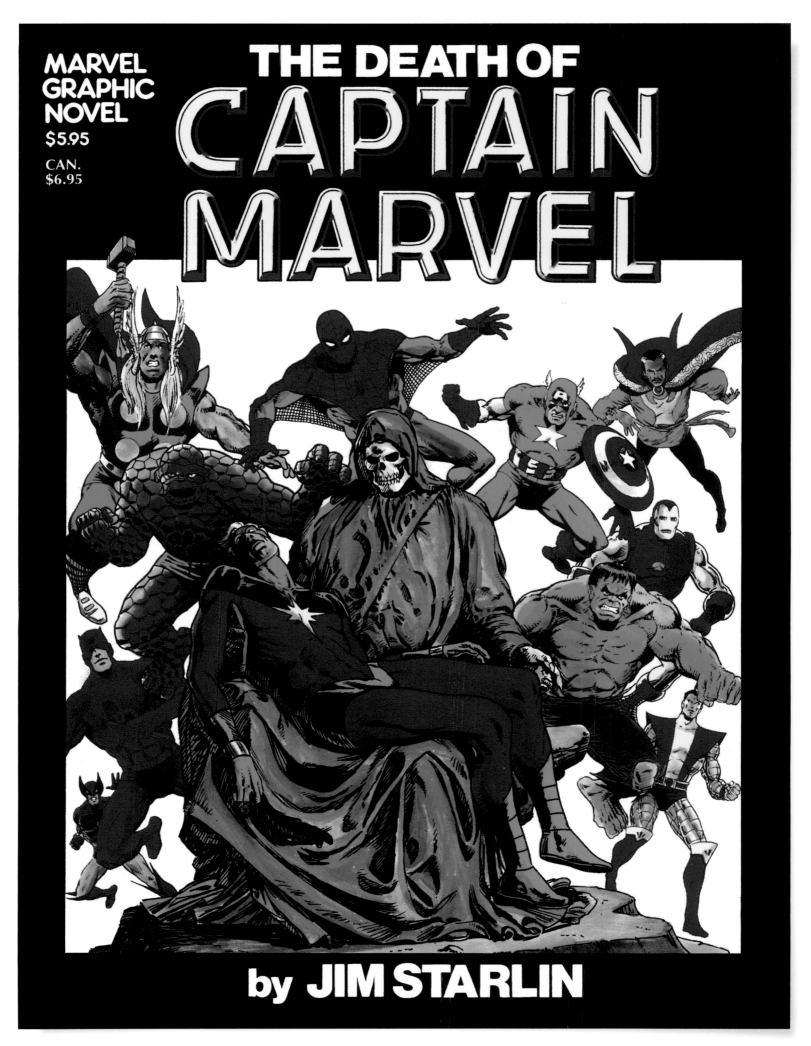

▲ *MARVEL GRAPHIC NOVEL 1: THE DEATH OF CAPTAIN MARVEL*

April 1982
Artist: Jim Starlin

When Marvel launched a graphic novel line, they needed something special to start the series. This epic tale was just the thing, with Jim Starlin writing and illustrating the final Captain Marvel story and doing the unthinkable—killing a major character in tragic and realistic circumstances. The cover is an atmospheric masterpiece, reflecting the intensity of the story.

◀ *CAPTAIN AMERICA #176*

August 1974
Artist: John Romita Sr.

The Watergate Affair touched even Marvel's heroes. This Romita cover reflects the post-Watergate soul-searching of many Americans. It features Steve Rogers turning his back on his role as Captain America. He felt betrayed after learning a "high-ranking political official" (the President) was the leader of the evil Secret Empire.

◀ *CAPTAIN AMERICA #180*

December 1974
Artist: Gil Kane

Captain America's soul-searching continued as he took on a new identity—Nomad, the man without a country. The cover is by Gil Kane, a Marvel veteran who produced many of the company's most famous covers. Kane's dynamic art style is used to full effect here, as the reader sees Steve Rogers leap into his new role.

◀ *CAPTAIN AMERICA* #230

February 1979
Artist: Ron Wilson

This powerful cover was illustrated by Ron Wilson, an artist most often associated with the Thing (he was the main artist on *Marvel-Two-in-One* and the Thing's first self-titled solo series). Wilson was used to drawing monstrously strong heroes, and here he manages to portray terrifying strength in a single punch. The reader can almost feel the impact of the Hulk's attack.

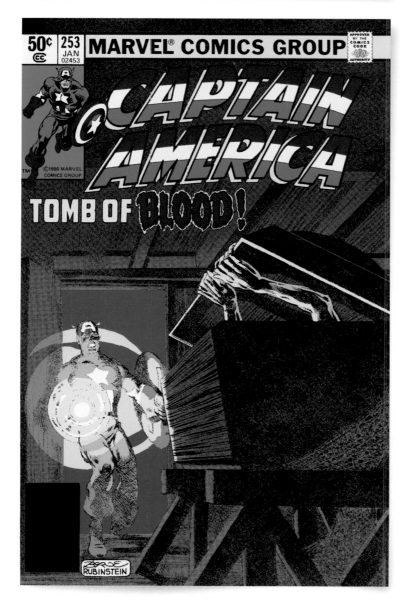

◀ *CAPTAIN AMERICA* #253

January 1981
Artist: John Byrne

John Byrne's spooky, atmospheric cover was influenced by some of the horror comics of the pre-Marvel era. This issue saw the return of Baron Blood, a British vampire who had backed the Axis Powers during World War II. Byrne's careful use of light and shadow was a sign of his increasing confidence as an artist.

◄ *DEFENDERS #4*

February 1973
Artists: Jim Starlin and John Buscema

Valkyrie made a dramatic return in this issue, riding the Black Knight's old horse. This time she had a new human host, a woman named Barbara Norris, and she was at the forefront of feminism, declaring that if the puny males couldn't defeat the bad guys, then she would. This version of Valkyrie became a mainstay of the *Defenders* and remained with the team for several years.

▲ *DOCTOR STRANGE #49*

October 1981
Artist: Marshall Rogers

Artist Marshall Rogers and writer Roger Stern had already worked together for a while before they brought their magic to Marvel's Sorcerer Supreme. Rogers excelled at stylish, otherworldly imagery and this cover shows off his amazing artwork perfectly.

▲ *DOCTOR STRANGE #51*

February 1982
Artist: Marshall Rogers

This second example of Rogers' work on *Doctor Strange* shows how well he conveyed action. Mystical battles were always a visual treat in *Doctor Strange* stories, ever since the days when Steve Ditko first illustrated the character. Rogers was one of the few who could match the sense of unreality that Ditko brought to his early tales.

▲ *INCREDIBLE HULK* #140

June 1971
Artist: Herb Trimpe

This Herb Trimpe classic was the cover to one of the greatest Hulk stories of all time, where the Hulk was shrunk into a microscopic world. Here he retained Bruce Banner's intelligence, was hailed as a hero, found true love with Jarella, and was about to live happily ever after—before it all went horribly wrong. The dynamic cover reflects a key moment in the story's heart-breaking climax, when the Hulk was seized and taken back to Earth.

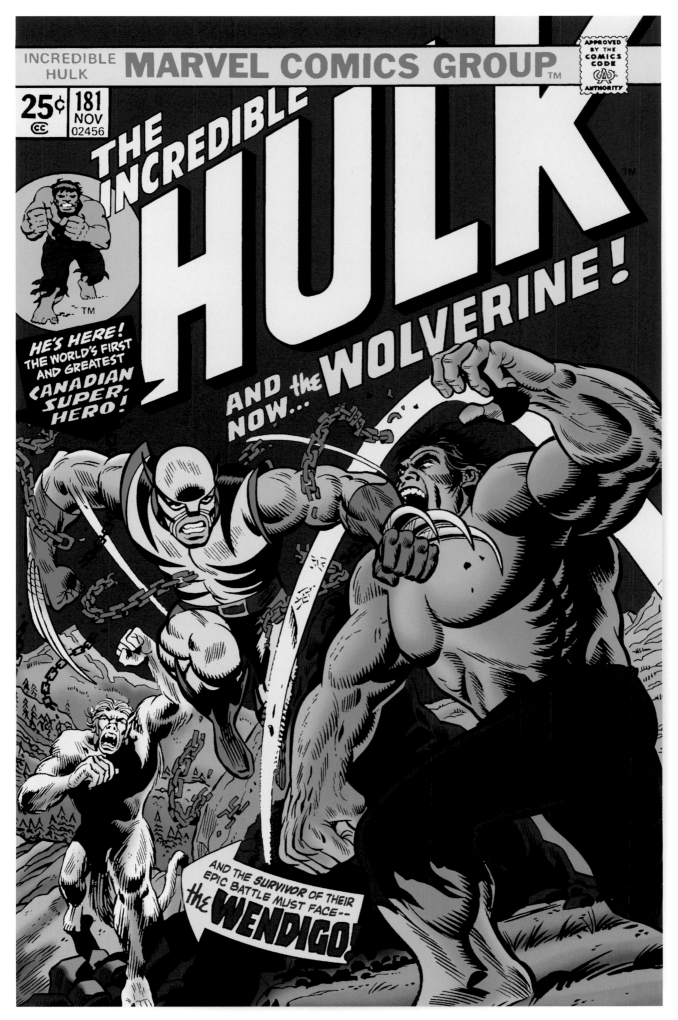

▲ *INCREDIBLE HULK* #181

November 1974
Artist: Herb Trimpe

"And now...the Wolverine!" It's hard to believe such a
simple tagline could signal the introduction of a hero
who would become one of Marvel's most popular characters.
Trimpe's cover is packed with action as the Canadian mutant
clashes with the Hulk. Wolverine later achieved fame as part of
the *New X-Men*, and his smackdowns with the Hulk became one
of the most anticipated clashes in the Marvel Universe.

▲ *IRON MAN #71*

November 1974
Artist: Ron Wilson

Iron Man poses have been the stock in trade of the armored hero's title, and it takes real skill to convey one in a fresh and interesting manner. Artist Ron Wilson manages to do just with his illustration of Tony Stark, in one of his most popular suits of armor, bursting out of the cover.

▲ *IRON MAN #118*

January 1979
Artist: Bob Layton

Bob Layton worked on *Iron Man* as co-writer, inker, and cover artist during one of its most memorable eras. He was the main artist on this dramatic cover, which shows the moment in the story when Tony Stark is thrown from S.H.I.E.L.D.'s Helicarrier. The mid-air change into his Iron Man armor makes for a tense and dramatic scene.

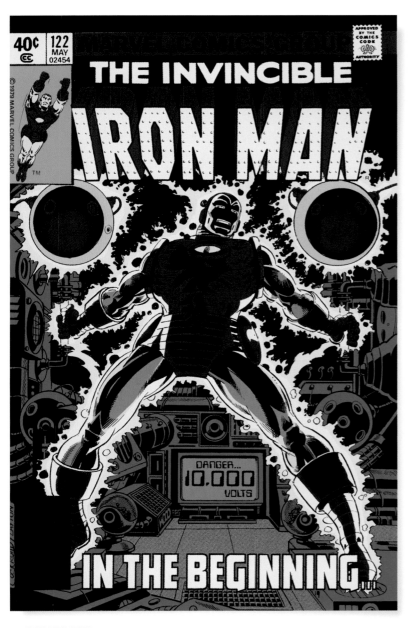

▲ IRON MAN #122

May 1979
Artist: Dave Cockrum

This Dave Cockrum cover is all about power and energy. The dramatic body pose of Iron Man, combined with colorist Ben Sean's electrifying colors, creates a real sense of tension as Iron Man is racked by high voltage. The inside story retold and updated Iron Man's origin.

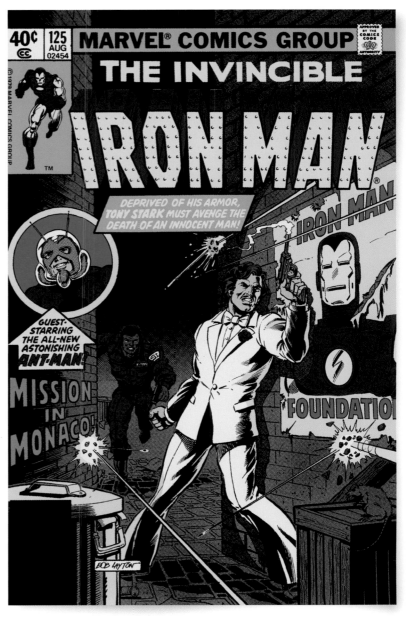

▲ IRON MAN #125

August 1979
Artist: Bob Layton

Bob Layton's cover for this issue is more spy-movie than Super Hero, showcasing the espionage angle that Layton (and co-writer David Michelinie) brought to Iron Man's adventures. It is also the first cover appearance of Jim Rhodes, who would later take on the role of Iron Man.

◀ *IRON MAN* #128

November 1979
Artist: Bob Layton

Often hailed as one of the greatest Marvel stories of all time, the "Demon in a Bottle!" storyline dealt with Tony Stark's alcoholism. It was a shockingly realistic story and needed a tough, hard-hitting cover. Bob Layton produced another exceptional piece—one often voted high on countdowns of *Iron Man's* best. The look of pain and horror on Stark's face, with the Iron Man helmet staring at him, is a haunting image.

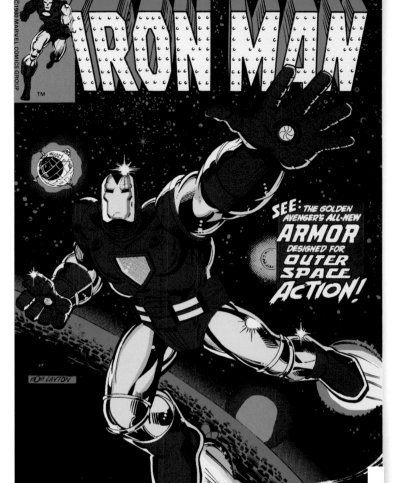

IRON MAN #142 ▶

January 1981
Artist: Bob Layton

These days Iron Man has countless armored suits at his disposal, but back in 1981 a change of armor was still a relatively new thing for the hero. This made Bob Layton's cover featuring a new space-faring armor all the more special.

IRON MAN #170 ▶

May 1983
Artist: Luke McDonnell

Jim Rhodes was revealed as the new Iron Man in this issue while Tony Stark relapsed into alcoholism. The prospect of a new Iron Man isn't only highlighted in the shadowy figure of Rhodes donning the helmet, but also in the array of previous armors in the background.

THOR #362

December 1985
Artist: Walt Simonson

One of the finest covers from Simonson's classic run, this issue proved to be Skurge the Executioner's finest hour. The cover highlighted his dramatic final moments, as the redeemed villain gave his life making a heroic last stand against overwhelming forces. His sacrifice allowed Thor and the Asgardian warriors to escape from Hela's dark realm.

▲ *FANTASTIC FOUR* #110

May 1971
Artist: John Buscema

The Fantastic Four's resident nanny (and witch) Agatha Harkness graces this cover, which showcases how the FF's adventures could cover magic as well as science fiction. John Buscema was the perfect replacement for Jack Kirby on the title, his dynamic style making sure the title remained one of Marvel's best.

▲ *FANTASTIC FOUR* #160

July 1975
Artist: Gil Kane

The Thing has always been one of the most popular characters in the Fantastic Four—and one that artists love to draw. Kane gives the Thing a real sense of strength in this scene, as the hero holds a twisted streetlamp as though it is a baseball bat while facing off against Arkon.

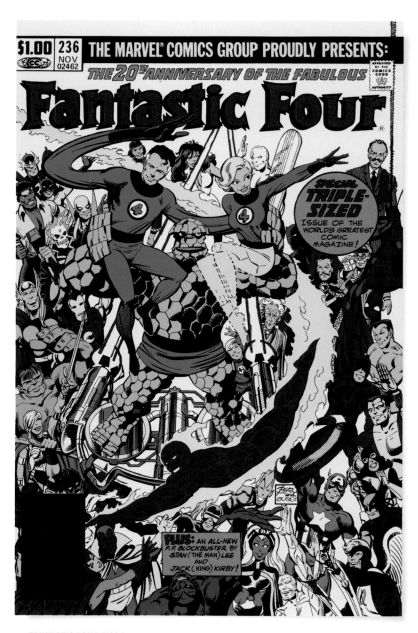

▲ *FANTASTIC FOUR #236*

November 1981
Artist: John Byrne

This issue came out on the 20th anniversary of both Marvel and the *Fantastic Four*. To celebrate the great occasion, John Byrne, who had started an iconic run on the title with issue #232, produced this stunning cover, which features all the greatest heroes of the Marvel Universe. Stan Lee even sneaks in for a cameo in the top right corner.

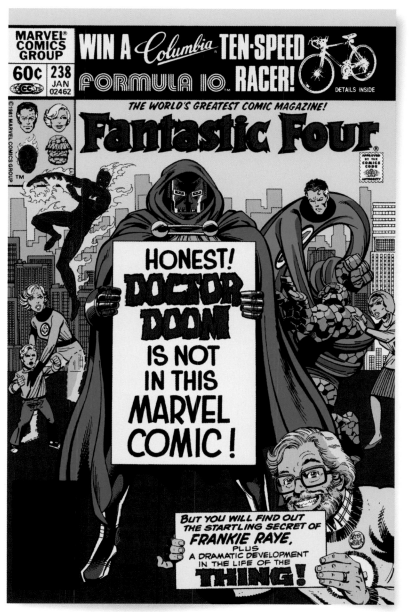

▲ *FANTASTIC FOUR #238*

January 1982
Artist: John Byrne

John Byrne brought a sense of fun and adventure back to Marvel's first family. This cover is a perfect example, with Doctor Doom breaking the fourth wall to warn readers that he isn't in the issue, and Byrne himself popping up to tell them how important this issue is.

◄ FANTASTIC FOUR #239

February 1982
Artist: John Byrne

A second Human Torch took to the skies in this issue as Johnny Storm's girlfriend Frankie Raye briefly joined him as another fiery hero. Byrne's cover has Frankie central to the image. The tagline of "the most unexpected guest-star of all time!" is no lie, as the Thing's Aunt Petunia makes her first appearance.

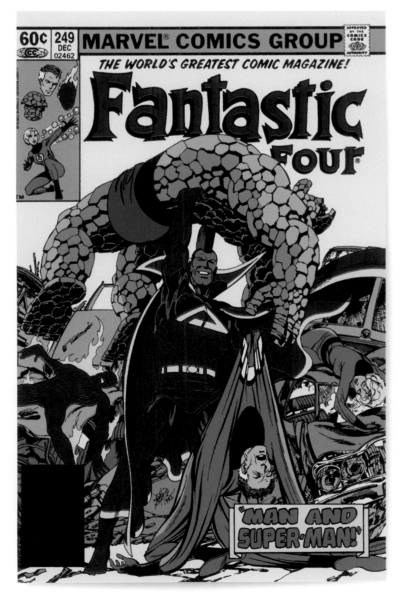

◄ FANTASTIC FOUR #249

December 1982
Artist: John Byrne

The Gladiator had first been seen in the pages of the *X-Men*, but he took on the Fantastic Four in this issue. Writer and artist John Byrne illustrated a dramatic cover showing the alien Super Hero standing triumphantly amidst a defeated FF.

◄ *FANTASTIC FOUR #258*

September 1983
Artists: John Byrne

John Byrne's covers often used strange angles or interesting images to make an effective cover. For this one he chose simplicity and power, and he made the villain the focus of the issue. Doom's armored hand (with his face reflected in it) tearing through the cover is a warning as to what was happening inside.

◄ *FANTASTIC FOUR #275*

February 1985
Artist: John Byrne

John Byrne showed his humorous side again with this issue, which features an editor who bears a strong resemblance to Marvel's own Stan Lee. The editor in the story, T.J. Vance, was threatening to print provocative photos of the She-Hulk—a problem that Bruce Banner's alter ego never had to deal with.

1.

2.

3.

JOHN BYRNE

Not only is John Byrne the artist behind some of Marvel's greatest comics and covers, he was also responsible for the rise in prominence of Wolverine. When Byrne joined writer Chris Claremont on the fledgling "All-New All-Different" X-Men in 1977, he persuaded the writer to give fellow Canadian Wolverine a greater role in the team. Byrne's interpretation of Wolverine made him one of Marvel's most popular heroes. Byrne is also renowned for his work on Fantastic Four; he brought a sense of adventure to the series not seen since the days of Lee and Kirby. His exceptional storytelling ability, coupled with a highly graphic but naturalistic style, has influenced a number of artists,

1. *UNCANNY X-MEN* #115

November 1978

One of John Byrne's early *Uncanny X-Men* covers (original art shown here) highlights the increased role Wolverine played thanks to Byrne's involvement. Byrne was a master of composition, creating an action-packed cover depicting Wolverine controlled by Sauron.

2. *ALPHA FLIGHT* #3

October 1983

Byrne was not scared to play with the graphic form. At a time when many artists took a conservative approach to cover design, Byrne explored new directions, such as this stark—and striking—use of black and white

3. *FANTASTIC FOUR* #244

July 1982

Byrne created a series of exceptional covers during his five-year run on *Fantastic Four*. In this powerful image of Frankie Raye being transformed into a herald of Galactus, Byrne instilled a real sense of the cosmic energy at work.

4. *UNCANNY X-MEN* #142

February 1981

This shocking cover showing Wolverine being killed by a Sentinel from "Days of Future Past" displayed Byrne's skill as a master of layout. It is a brutal but eye-catching image of futuristic versions of Wolverine and Storm.

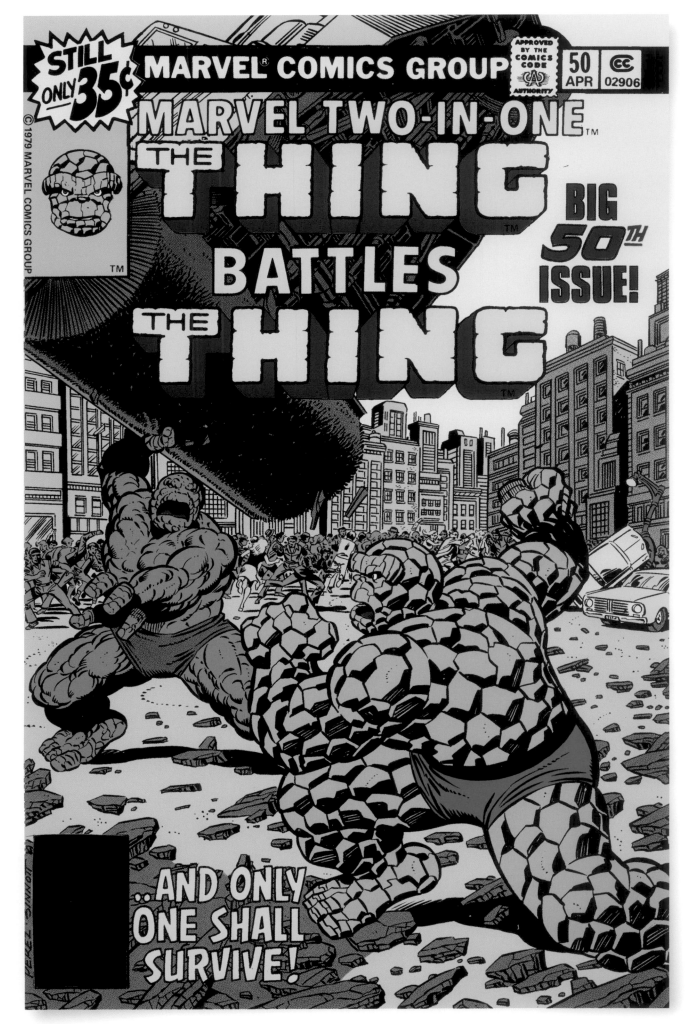

▲ *MARVEL TWO-IN-ONE #50*

April 1979
Artist: George Pérez

George Pérez handled the cover art for this epic that was
written and illustrated by John Byrne. The cover shows the
key scene of the issue as the modern-day Thing traveled
back in time in an attempt to cure himself of his mutation.
He ends up facing, and fighting, his younger and more
monstrous self. The tagline told the truth—it was
a meeting only one Thing would survive.

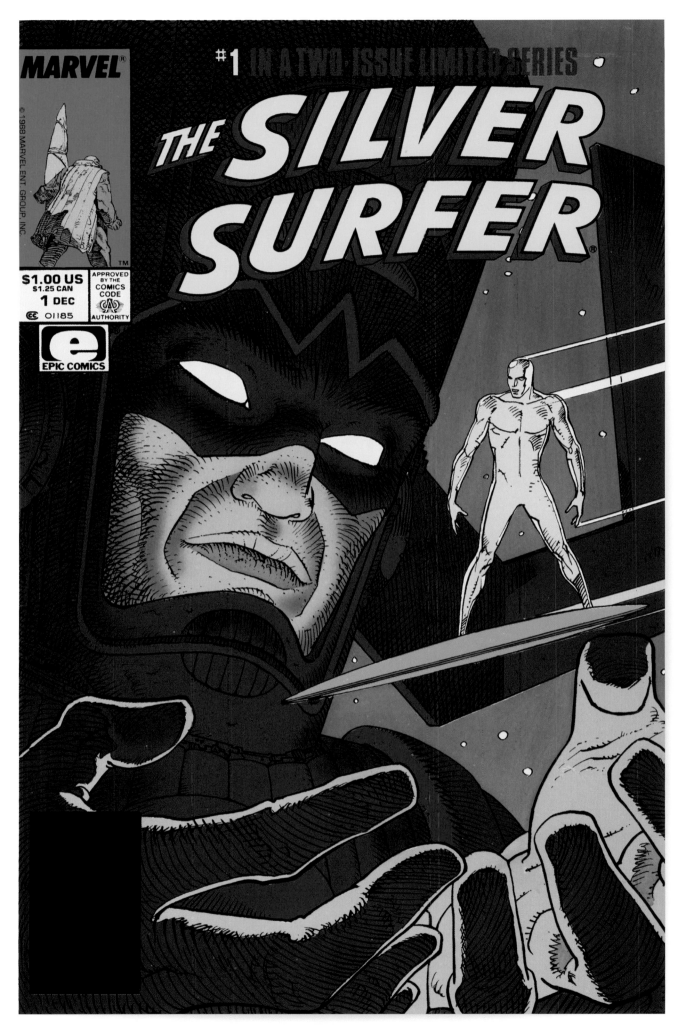

▲ *SILVER SURFER* #1

December 1988
Artist: Moebius

In the world of comics, artists don't come much bigger
than Moebius. An award-winning part of the European
comic scene, Moebius teamed up with writer Stan Lee to
create the two-issue story "Parable." Moebius produced a
truly godlike Galactus and brought out the alien-outsider in
the Silver Surfer, the subtle colors adding to the grandeur
of the scene. The series went on to win an Eisner Award.

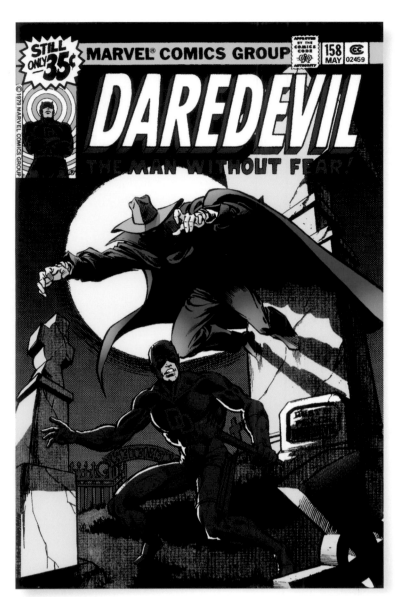

◄ *DAREDEVIL #158*

May 1979
Artist: Frank Miller

For his first *Daredevil* cover, Frank Miller held back slightly from the action-packed noir style that would soon make *Daredevil* one of the most popular comics of the decade. Miller grew in confidence while working on this series, quickly becoming one of the medium's top creators.

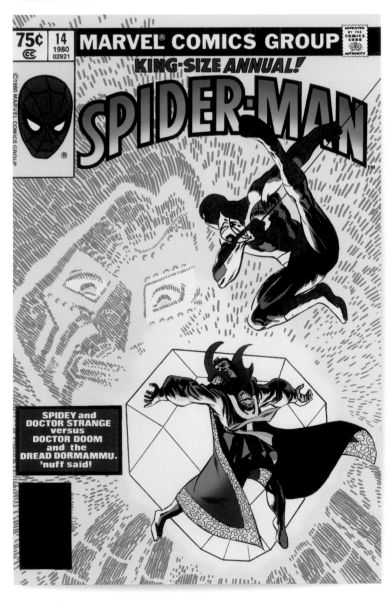

◄ *AMAZING SPIDER-MAN ANNUAL #14*

October 1980
Artist: Frank Miller

Frank Miller worked on covers for Marvel before becoming a writer and artist on the interiors. This cover is a clear example of his early style, displaying a bold use of color and shadow. It also highlights Miller's ability to infuse a powerful sense of movement and energy to his art.

DAREDEVIL #168 ►

January 1981
Artist: Frank Miller

The cover of this issue helped Frank Miller put his mark on *Daredevil*. As well as writing and illustrating the issue, Miller introduced Elektra, a new character who was the lost love of Matt Murdock's life and a deadly assassin. It became one of the most popular Marvel stories of all time. Unfortunately, however, Elektra's name was spelled incorrectly on the cover.

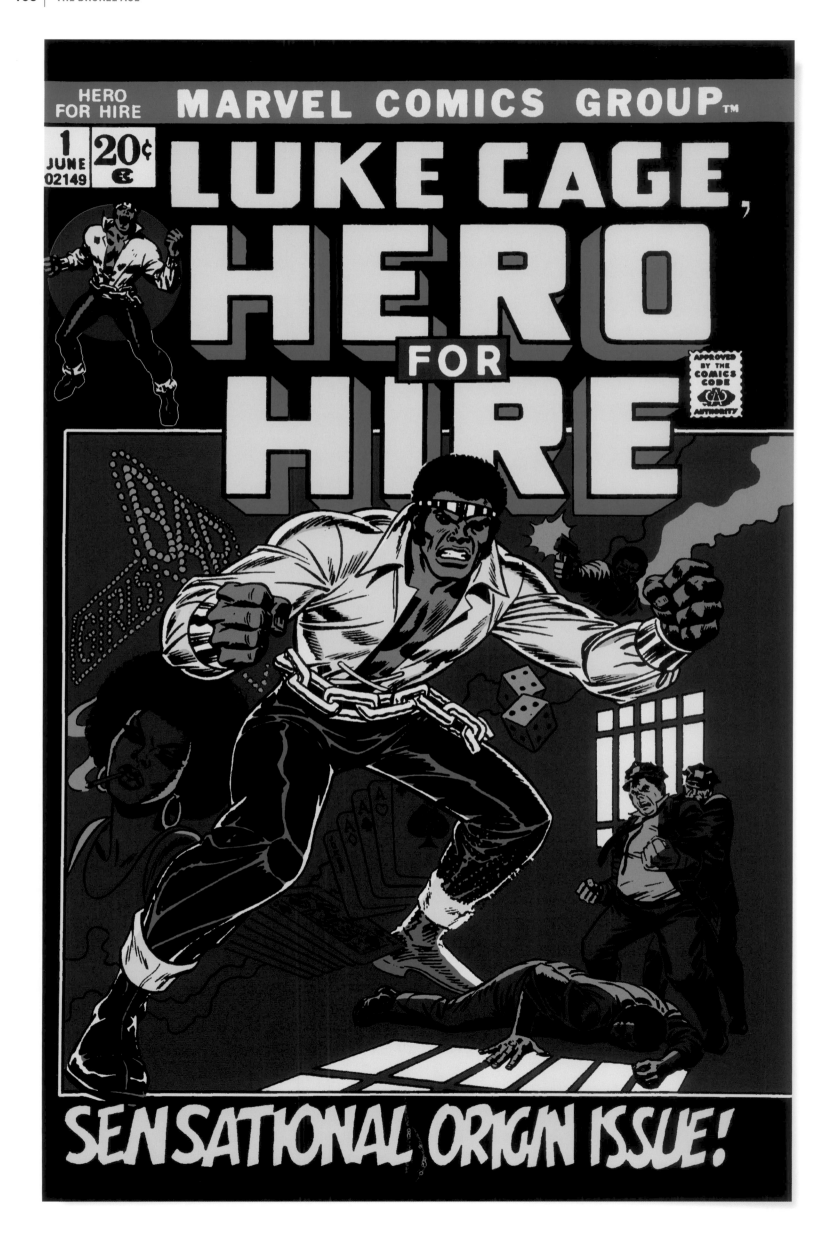

◀ *LUKE CAGE, HERO FOR HIRE #1*

June 1972
Artist: George Tuska

Blaxploitation movies were hugely popular
in the early 1970s and Marvel added their
own comic-book take on the genre with
Luke Cage, Hero for Hire. Luke was one of
the first African-American Super Heroes
to star in his own comic, as Marvel again
pushed back barriers with their titles. The
cover is more like a movie poster than a
regular comic cover, showing key scenes
from the issue and Luke's troubled past.

▲ *IRON FIST #14*

August 1977
Artist: Dave Cockrum

A big cultural trend in the early 1970s was
the martial arts craze, following the release
of Bruce Lee's movie *Enter the Dragon*. One of
Marvel's unique takes on the genre was *Iron Fist*.
This classic cover isn't just an accomplished work
of comic cover art though—it also marks the first
appearance of the character Sabretooth.

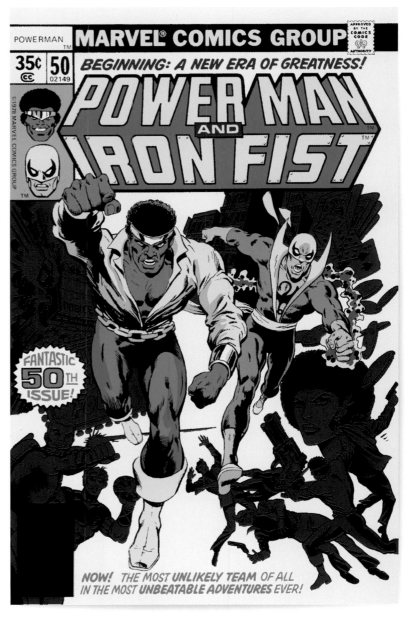

▲ *POWER MAN AND IRON FIST #50*

April 1978
Artist: Dave Cockrum

Iron Fist and *Luke Cage: Power Man* (*Luke Cage,
Hero for Hire* had been renamed) became one title
with this issue and one of the best-loved comics of
the time. Dave Cockrum's cool cover montage has
echoes of Luke's first issue and perfectly suits
the heroes' realistic street-level adventures.

TOMB OF DRACULA #10

July 1973
Artist: Gil Kane

Of all the horror comics to come out of this era, *Tomb of Dracula* enjoyed the longest life and the best critical reception. Most issues were written by Marv Wolfman and illustrated by Gene Colan. However, Gil Kane—arguably at his peak—handled the cover art for this issue, which depicts the dramatic first appearance of Blade, the Vampire Slayer.

▲ *MARVEL SPOTLIGHT #2*

February 1972
Artist: Neal Adams

When the Comics Code Authority began to relax its guidelines to allow horror comics once more, Marvel wasted little time in turning its attention to horror-related heroes. Jack Russell, aka the Werewolf by Night, was one of the first, with Neal Adams depicting Jack's painful transformation into the werewolf in a multi-frame cover image.

▲ *MARVEL SPOTLIGHT #5*

August 1972
Artist: Mike Ploog

Ghost Rider—perhaps one of Marvel's coolest looking heroes—made his debut this issue, courtesy of artist Mike Ploog and writer Gary Friedrich, aided and abetted by editor Roy Thomas. Ploog's action-packed cover illustration introduced the character's famous motorcycle and helped to establish the debutant as "The most Supernatural Super Hero of all!"

ADVENTURE INTO FEAR #11 ▶

December 1972
Artist: Neal Adams

This atmospheric Neal Adams cover shows an early appearance of the monstrous Man-Thing. The creature had first appeared in *Savage Tales* issue #1 (May 1971), but soon gained his own full-color series. The Adams cover reflects how, since the relaxation of the Comics Code, Marvel were able to feature mystical elements such as the pentagram.

▲ *TALES OF THE ZOMBIE* #1

July 1973
Artist: Boris Vallejo

Marvel created a new magazine line that didn't come under the scrutiny of the Comics Code Authority. Cover artist Boris Vallejo was one of the best fantasy artists in the business, combining horror and sensuality to great effect, as demonstrated here with his depiction of Simon Garth, the Zombie.

▲ *DRACULA LIVES* #1

August 1973
Artist: Boris Vallejo

The greatest vampire of all gained his own magazine shortly after the successful launch of *Tomb of Dracula* in the previous month. Boris Vallejo's stunning painted artwork graced the cover. The more adult-oriented content—indicated by the sophisticated painterly covers—proved to be a big hit for Marvel.

▲ *RAMPAGING HULK* #1

January 1977
Artist: Ken Barr

Marvel also gave some of their Super Heroes the magazine
treatment. The Hulk was one of the first to make the transition,
and the fantastic painted cover by Ken Barr makes the green
Goliath look more realistic and menacing than ever, with him
staring rangrily out at the reader as well as the soldiers in the
foreground. The title was an anthology, featuring harder-edged,
more adult stories than those in the regular comic bocks.

▲ *MARVEL PREVIEW #4*

January 1976
Artist: Gray Morrow

Star-Lord started out a solo adventurer but would later be the leader of a new incarnation of the Guardians of the Galaxy. This issue was his first appearance, revealing just how he ended up in space. The painterly style of Gray Morrow's cover was heavily influenced by his other job— illustrating paperback book covers.

AMAZING ADVENTURES #18 ▶

May 1973
Artist: John Romita Sr.

Marvel created an action-packed, comic book follow-up to H.G. Wells' novel *War of the Worlds*, with John Romita Sr. producing a futuristic cover for the debut issue. It shows the hero, Killraven, in a post-apocalyptic landscape ravaged by Martian war-machines.

MARVEL PRESENTS #3 ▶

February 1976
Artist: John Romita Sr.

Decades before a new incarnation of the Guardians of the Galaxy took to the big screen, the original team enjoyed futuristic adventures. The Guardians first appeared in *Marvel Super Heroes* issue #18 in 1969. They remained the stars of *Marvel Presents* until the series finished with issue #12, and John Romita Sr. producing one of the most striking early covers.

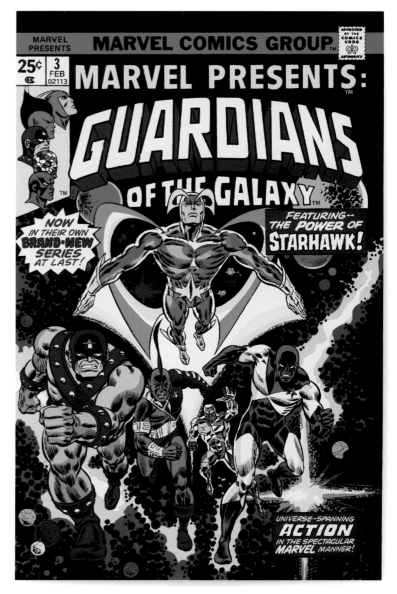

NOVA #12

August 1977

Artist: John Buscema

Before the computer age, cover creation was a far more hands-on job. In the case of *Nova* issue #12, artist John Buscema would have started the process with a rough layout showing character placement in conjunction with the logo (1). Once that had been approved by Marvel's Art Editor, he would then move on to more detailed pencils (2, 3), before passing the art on to an inker—in this case, Frank Giacoia—to add black line to his pencils (4). Editorial would then make a high-quality copy of the artwork—complete with logo and text added—for a colorist to finish the work. The completed work (5) would then be approved by Marvel's editorial, before it was sent to the printers with the rest of the issue.

1. Sketch
2. Pencil
3. Pencil
4. Inked pencil
5. Final cover

1.

2.

3.

4.

5.

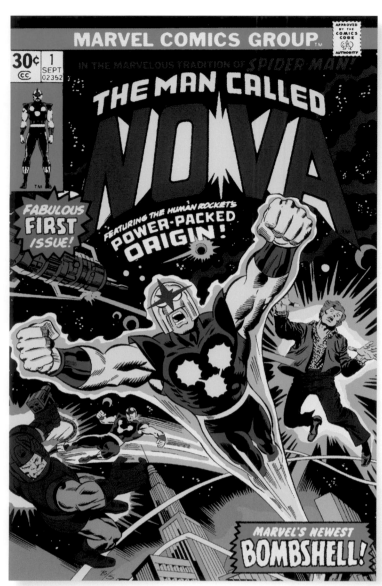

◀ *NOVA* #1

September 1976
Artist: Rich Buckler

Marvel released a number of new titles in the mid-1970s and *Nova* proved to be one of the most popular. Rich Buckler's cover showcases Nova's origin as the star-spanning cosmic hero. The top strap highlights the fact that Marvel were trying to create another teenage Super Hero in the tradition of Spider-Man.

◀ *MS. MARVEL* #1

January 1977
Artist: John Romita Sr.

Carol Danvers was revealed as Ms. Marvel, a new female Super Hero, in this issue. In the early 1970s, female Super Heroes were still relatively few—something Marvel tried to change with Ms. Marvel and Spider-Woman. This classy cover was the perfect montage to attract new readers to the title.

MACHINE MAN #1–4 ▶

October 1984–January 1985
Artist: Barry Windsor-Smith

Barry Windsor-Smith originally made his name as the artist on *Conan the Barbarian*. His return to Marvel in the 1980s resulted in a great series of covers. These four covers show the Machine Man's growth during the story (which was set in the year 2020) and the fact that he was literally rebuilt, having been found on a scrap heap. It was a tale that saw the hero grow from being little more than a broken android into a true machine man.

◀ *AMAZING SPIDER-MAN #87*

August 1970
Artist: John Romita Sr.

Soap-opera drama has always been a big part of Spider-Man's success—and this cover has that in spades. With Romita as artist, Spidey had become Marvel's most popular character. This issue showcases Romita's talent for combining drama with super heroics, as Peter reveals his true identity to his friends.

◀ *AMAZING SPIDER-MAN #96*

May 1971
Artist: Gil Kane

In this classic Gil Kane piece, Marvel pushed the boundaries of the medium—this time by dealing with the subject of drug abuse. The Comics Code Authority refused to give this issue its seal of approval, but Marvel published it anyway, using Harry Osborn's addiction to highlight the dangers of drug use.

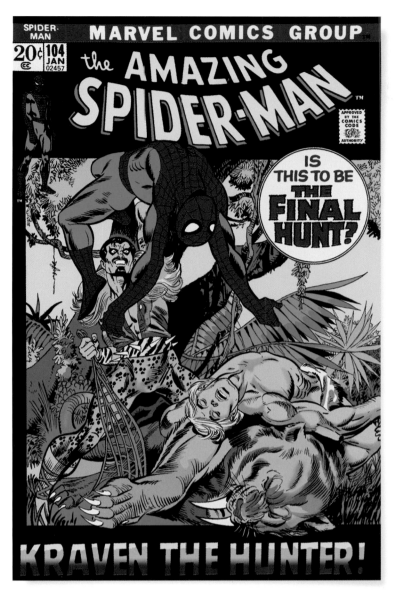

◄ *AMAZING SPIDER-MAN* #104

January 1972
Artist: Gil Kane

Gil Kane demonstrated a real flair for design in his work, as this Spider-Man and Kraven cover shows. Indeed, it was Kane who was responsible for the boxed-off-image layout of many of the covers produced in this era, during which he was the company's leading artist.

◄ *AMAZING SPIDER-MAN* #112

September 1972
Artist: John Romita Sr.

This classic Romita cover shows the webslinger turning his back on his heroic duties, as rioters create havoc on the streets of New York (reflecting the period of civil unrest in the '70s). The real reason for Spidey's malaise however, was revealed inside the comic: concern for his Aunt May's health, in the first part of a powerful story.

◄ *AMAZING SPIDER-MAN* #121

June 1973
Artist: John Romita Sr.

John Romita Sr.'s cover was designed to tantalize fans: Someone Spidey knew was going to die, but who would it be? The somewhat shocking answer was Gwen Stacy, thrown to her doom by the Green Goblin. This issue, and the one that followed it, signified a change not only in Spidey's life but also in Marvel's comics. If Gwen Stacy, one of the most popular supporting characters in the Marvel Universe, could be killed, it meant that no one was safe.

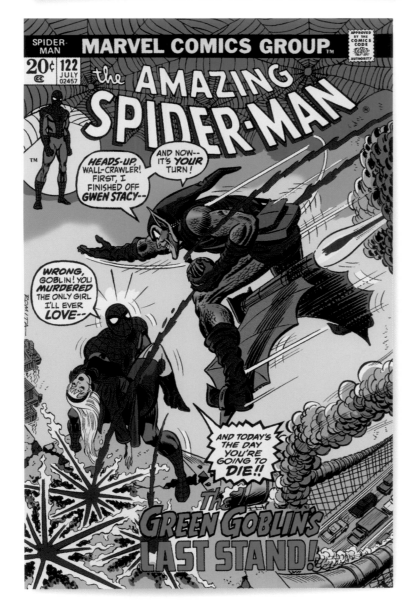

◄ *AMAZING SPIDER-MAN* #122

July 1973
Artist: John Romita Sr.

The powerful cover image of the webslinger carrying Gwen Stacy's body made this issue a must-have for Spidey fans. As the grief-stricken hero declares that her killer will pay, the cover seemed to promise the vengeance they wanted, too. Although Romita produced another outstanding cover, it was Gil Kane who got to draw the story, which appeared to show another death—this time, the Green Goblin's.

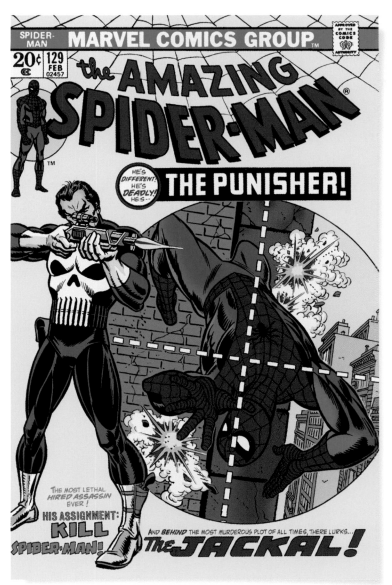

◄ *AMAZING SPIDER-MAN* #129

February 1974
Artist: Gil Kane

The Punisher made his debut this issue, with Gil Kane providing an amazing cover of Spidey caught in the vigilante's crosshairs. John Romita Sr. inked Kane's cover, while Ross Andru illustrated the interior. The Punisher started out as a villain, but over the years he slowly became more of an anti-hero—and one of Marvel's most popular characters. In this issue, the Punisher was manipulated by the Jackal into believing that Spider-Man was a criminal.

◄ *AMAZING SPIDER-MAN* #131

April 1974
Artist: Gil Kane

This might well be the weirdest Spider-Man cover of all time— and one of the strangest stories. Gil Kane handled the cover art showing Doctor Octopus about to marry Peter Parker's Aunt May. It was crazy, but true. However, it was a marriage of convenience for Doc Ock—the villain only wanted to get his arms on an island May had inherited, which just happened to house a nuclear power plant.

▲ *AMAZING SPIDER-MAN* #135

August 1974
Artist: John Romita Sr.

The shadowy image of a tarantula is used to nice effect on this cover, separating the quick-fire images that reflect the key moments in the story—including the return of the Punisher. The art conveys the soap-opera-style drama of Spidey's adventures and also the uniqueness of his enemies.

▲ *AMAZING SPIDER-MAN* #136

September 1974
Artist: John Romita Sr.

With its excellent use of coloring and layout, this John Romita masterpiece shows Harry Osborn in the role of the Green Goblin for the first time, pitting him against his closest friend, Peter Parker. The use of both friends in their civilian identities below their alter egos highlights the tense action of the issue.

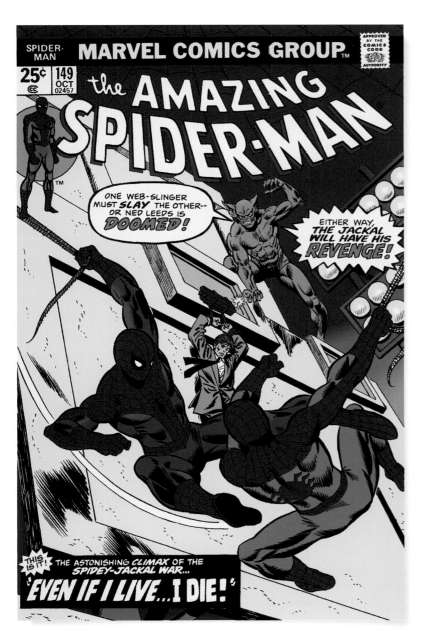

▲ *AMAZING SPIDER-MAN #149*

October 1975
Artist: Gil Kane

What Spidey fan could resist buying this
now classic issue after seeing its stunning
Gil Kane cover? The webslinger met his
match in this issue—literally. He was
forced to fight his own clone—with the
winner still not sure whether he was
the real Spider-Man or just a copy.

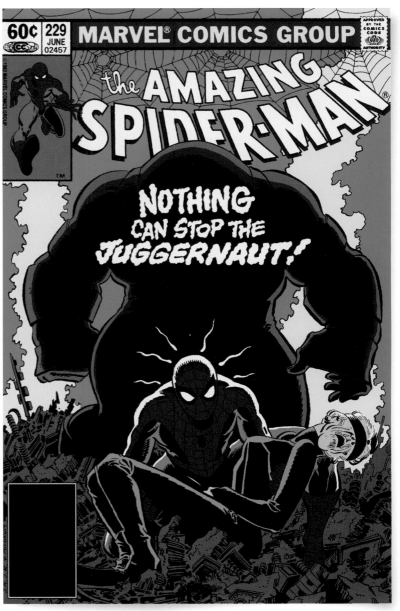

▲ *AMAZING SPIDER-MAN #229*

June 1982
Artist: John Romita Jr.

This is often voted one of the all-time
great Spider-Man stories. Writer Roger
Stern and artist John Romita Jr.
teamed up to pit Spidey against the
Juggernaut. The cover proves the
younger Romita had all the skills of
his father when it came to creating
brilliant, eye-catching covers.

1.

2.

3.

JOHN ROMITA SR.

John Romita Sr. is one of the most important artists ever to grace Marvel's hallowed halls. Not only did his clear, stylish artwork make Spider-Man a household name, but his role as Marvel's Art Editor led him to help visualize a vast swath of Marvel heroes—including Wolverine, the Punisher, and Luke Cage—and produce some of the company's most iconic covers. Before he started on Spider-Man, Romita had mostly drawn romance titles for DC Comics. He brought this style (good-looking characters created with a clean line) over to his Super-Hero work. Taking over *Amazing Spider-Man* from Steve Ditko, Romita naturally made all of the characters better looking, and also created Spidey's girlfriend, Mary Jane Watson. The comic soon became Marvel's best-selling title.

1. *AMAZING SPIDER-MAN* #136

September 1974

This black-and-white cover mock-up is a great example of Romita's fine talents as a draftsman. Romita skillfully conveys the anger in the figures of Peter and Harry, while the dramatic layout adds a real sense of danger to the scene.

2. *DAREDEVIL* #16

May 1966

Stan Lee used this cover as a test piece to see if Romita could handle illustrating the webslinger. The motion of the two heroes clashing on the cover, and the stunning interior work, proved to Lee that Romita was the perfect choice to follow Ditko.

3. *OUR LOVE STORY* #1

October 1969

Romita had cut his teeth on romance comics and continued to illustrate the occasional issue while working for Marvel. As this cover shows, Romita was a master of conveying emotion, as well as making his characters both attractive and realistic.

4. *AMAZING SPIDER-MAN* #123

August 1973

During his stint as Marvel's Art Editor, Romita helped create a number of heroes, including Luke Cage. The new character soon guest-starred in *Amazing Spider-Man*, and Romita combined perspective and action to create a dramatic cover.

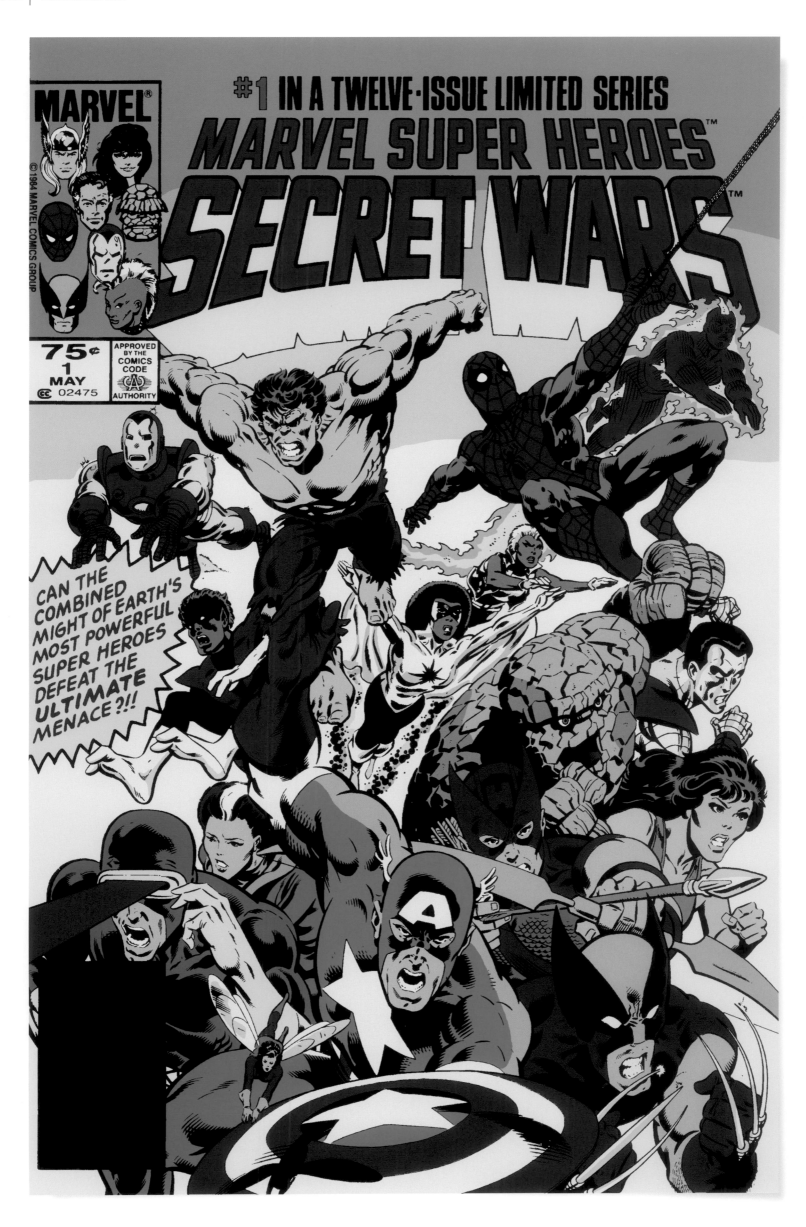

AMAZING SPIDER-MAN #252 ▶

May 1984
Artist: Ron Frenz

Frenz's striking image was a homage to Jack Kirby's original *Amazing Fantasy* issue #15 cover *(see p50)*. This Spidey issue came out the same month as the *Secret Wars* series, and it tantalized fans by showing Spider-Man in a new black costume, leaving them hungry to find out how he came to be wearing it.

MARVEL SUPER HEROES SECRET WARS #8 ▶

December 1984
Artist: Mike Zeck

Readers had to wait until issue #8 of *Secret Wars* to learn about Spidey's new costume and how he got it. Mike Zeck's cover not only showed the webslinger dressed in black, but also hinted at the devastation caused by the wars.

◀ MARVEL SUPER HEROES SECRET WARS #1

May 1984
Artist: Mike Zeck

It was the biggest crossover series of the decade as Marvel's great heroes were transported to the distant planet of Battleworld to fight their greatest enemies. The cover was by Mike Zeck, who also illustrated the 12-part series. It was the first epic to bring together so many characters in such a long series, and Zeck's artistic expertise truly brings the exciting cast to life in this piece.

▲ *WHAT IF?* #1

February 1977
Artist: Jim Craig

The *What If?* series was a simple but brilliant concept. It introduced readers to parallel Earths where some of Marvel's most important storylines had decidedly different outcomes. Jim Craig's cover showing Spidey as part of the Fantastic Five was an intriguing concept—and a great way to start the series.

▲ *MARVEL TEAM-UP* #65

January 1978
Artist: George Pérez

Captain Britain made his first US appearance in this issue, alongside Spider-Man. George Pérez produced an exciting cover to introduce the hero to a new audience. Captain Britain's appearance led to a traditional comic-book misunderstanding with the two heroes coming to blows before teaming up to stop their true enemy, Arcade.

MARVEL FANFARE #6 ▶

January 1983
Artist: P. Craig Russell

Marvel Fanfare was a prestige-format Marvel comic that showcased the work of the very best artists. Even by the high standards of the series, this P. Craig Russell cover of the Scarlet Witch and Spider-Man is something special. Russell has only produced a limited amount of comic-book work, but his contributions have been outstanding.

▲ *THE NEW MUTANTS #18*

August 1984
Artist: Bill Sienkiewicz

One of the most-loved eras of *The New Mutants* started when Bill Sienkiewicz joined writer Chris Claremont on the book. Sienkiewicz had already been working for Marvel for several years, but it was during his work on *The New Mutants* that he really developed his famous expressionistic style. The cover of his first issue signified the start of the classic "Demon Bear" saga and focused on Dani Moonstar (aka Mirage), with help from Sienkiewicz's haunting portrait.

▲ *WOLVERINE* #1

September 1982
Artist: Frank Miller

Wolverine's first, long-awaited series saw one of Marvel's
hottest artists, Frank Miller, team with writer Chris Claremont.
Miller's love of Japanese manga and film was reflected in the
storyline, while his cover art showcases his exceptional ability
to add a sense of realism to the toughest of characters.

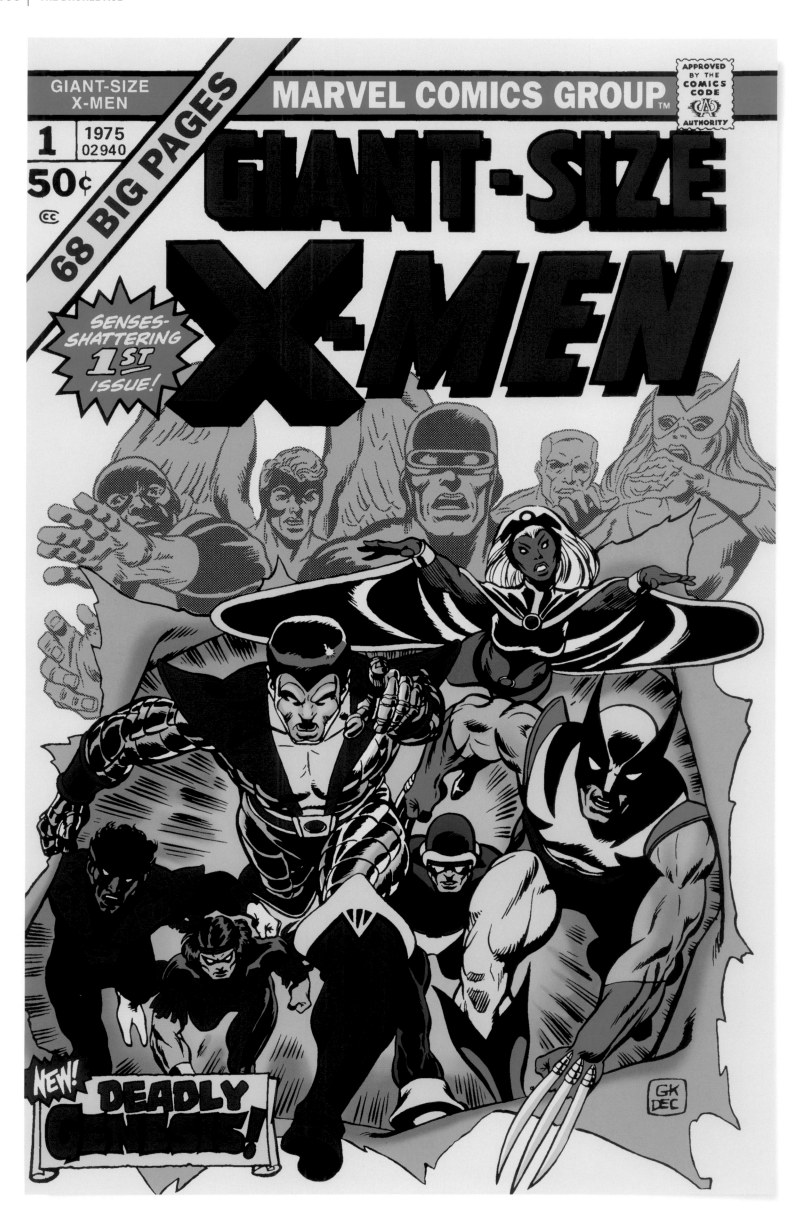

◄ *GIANT-SIZE X-MEN #1*

May 1975
Artists: Gil Kane and Dave Cockrum

Few comics have changed the very nature of a company the way the new, more international X-Men title changed Marvel. Thanks to the new team's success, the X-Men didn't just become a comic series, but an entire franchise—and it all began with this bumper issue and one spectacular, and much copied, cover. Gil Kane's stylish and striking cover (inked by the new team's co-creator, Dave Cockrum) shows the all-new X-Men bursting out, as the old team look on in shock.

▲ *X-MEN #94*

August 1975
Artists: Gil Kane and Dave Cockrum

Following the success of *Giant-Size X-Men*, the team's regular book was started up again, continuing the numbering from the previous incarnation of the team. Dave Cockrum and Gil Kane again joined forces to create a dramatic cover showing the villainous Count Nefaria sending the mutant team to their doom. Writer Chris Claremont also joined on this issue.

▲ *X-MEN #100*

August 1976
Artist: Dave Cockrum

The cover of this centenary issue shows the original X-Men team facing off against their successors. Writer Chris Claremont was starting to come into his own after six issues. The cover demonstrates how, alongside Dave Cockrum (and later John Byrne), Claremont was developing and expanding the X-Men universe.

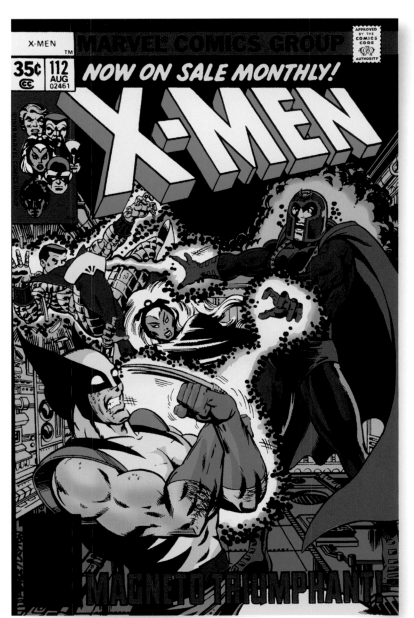

▲ *X-MEN* #111

June 1978
Artist: Dave Cockrum

While the new *X-Men* comic was proving successful, it was only when penciller John Byrne joined the book (with issue #108) that the series became the publishing juggernaut that it is today. Dave Cockrum continued to contribute some outstanding covers for the team though, including this one, showing the X-Men trapped in a mysterious circus freak-show.

▲ *X-MEN* #112

August 1982
Artists: Dave Cockrum and George Pérez

Dave Cockrum and George Pérez worked together to create this tense cover, while John Byrne handled the interior art. Byrne also suggested to writer Chris Claremont that Wolverine could be given a larger role in the team. So on the cover, Wolverine takes center stage—but his Adamantium skeleton proved all too easy for Magneto to control.

◄ *X-MEN* #101

October 1976
Artist: Dave Cockrum

With the new X-Men team edgier than the previous incarnation, it was time to give Jean Grey (Marvel Girl) a makeover. When Jean Grey died and came back as Phoenix, it not only inspired one of the most striking *X-Men* covers of all time, but it also created a character who would take the lead in many of Marvel's best-loved X-Men-related epics. In many ways, this cover signifies when the "All-New, All-Different" X-Men really started to come into their own.

▲ *UNCANNY X-MEN #124*

August 1979
Artist: Dave Cockrum

Marvel had added "Uncanny" to the title from issue #114. This issue explored Colossus' Soviet background when he was brainwashed by the villain Arcade into believing he was a Russian hero called the Proletarian rather than a member of the X-Men. In a world in the midst of the Cold War, the image of Colossus in Soviet insignia was powerful and topical.

▲ *UNCANNY X-MEN #130*

February 1980
Artist: John Romita Jr.

Dazzler had originally been conceived as part of a multimedia cross-promotion between Marvel and Casablanca Records. The record company planned to launch the career of a singer that they would name Dazzler just as Marvel produced a comic about her. However, ultimately the singer only came to exist in the world of *X-Men* comics. The cover of Dazzler's debut appearance is a mash-up of X-Men and disco, with disco lights even added to the logo.

▲ *UNCANNY X-MEN #132*

April 1980
Artist: John Byrne

The "Hellfire Club" saga remains one of
the most important stories in the X-Men's
history. This cover highlights the unique-
looking villains of the Hellfire Club (a social
club with a slightly sinister agenda), the like
of which had never been seen in a Marvel
comic before. By this point *Uncanny X-Men*
was winning awards and going from strength
to strength each month.

▲ *UNCANNY X-MEN #133*

May 1980
Artist: John Byrne

Wolverine had gradually become the most
popular mutant Super Hero during Claremont
and Byrne's run, but this was the issue in
which he really cut loose. The image, showing
Wolverine taking on the Hellfire Club's security,
was the first time the hero had the cover to
himself. It certainly wouldn't be the last.

◀ *UNCANNY X-MEN #134*

June 1980
Artist: John Byrne

When Jean Grey gives in to the darkside, she is remade by the Hellfire Club as their Black Queen. She takes center stage on this cover, surrounded by the Phoenix flame. The drama intensified in this issue, and the cover is all about dramatic color—the powerful red and yellow reflecting the fiery danger the X-Men team faced.

◀ *UNCANNY X-MEN #135*

July 1980
Artist: John Byrne

Jean Grey's fall continued in this issue with the hero becoming Dark Phoenix. The powerful cover shows a supercharged and insane-looking Jean crushing the X-Men logo, clearly signifying how she was hell-bent on destroying everything in her path. It was a sign of the drama within, as the X-Men had to face one of their own who had now become their deadliest enemy.

◀ *UNCANNY X-MEN* #136

August 1980
Artist: John Byrne

The "Dark Phoenix" saga reached its penultimate chapter this issue with an emotional cover. The image of Cyclops holding what seems to be the corpse of Jean Grey in his arms (she is in fact, unconscious) is an exceptionally powerful one, as is Cyclops' agonized expression. While the main pose has been used before, this is one of the most famous instances of its use.

◀ *UNCANNY X-MEN* #137

September 1980
Artist: John Byrne

The tagline says it all: "Phoenix Must Die!" The "Dark Phoenix" saga came to its tragic conclusion in this special double-size issue as the X-Men and Jean Grey fought for her life. The iconic image of Cyclops and Jean Grey (in her original Marvel Girl costume) making a last stand remains burned into every X-Men fan's memory.

▲ *X-MEN* #138

October 1980
Artist: John Byrne

John Byrne's run as *X-Men* artist produced many classic covers and stories, but this simple cover remains a highlight. A fitting epilogue to the "Dark Phoenix" saga, it featured Cyclops quitting the team as he tried to come to terms with the death of Jean Grey. Byrne's layout has been used many times since, while the backdrop of old covers illustrated Cyclops' long history with the team.

▲ *UNCANNY X-MEN* #139

November 1980
Artist: John Byrne

After the grim trauma of the "Dark Phoenix" saga, it was time to shake things up at Xavier's Mansion. Kitty Pryde was just the person to add some fresh, new blood to the team. This cover, showing the teenage Kitty surrounded by the X-Men in peril, heralded a time of change for the title.

UNCANNY X-MEN #141 ▶

January 1981
Artist: John Byrne

Even by the high standards of John Byrne, the cover to the first part of the classic story "Days of Future Past" is something special. The image of a desperate and aged Wolverine next to a grown-up Kate Pryde is a startling one, especially with the list of dead or captured X-Men behind them. It is a cover that has often been copied, but never bettered.

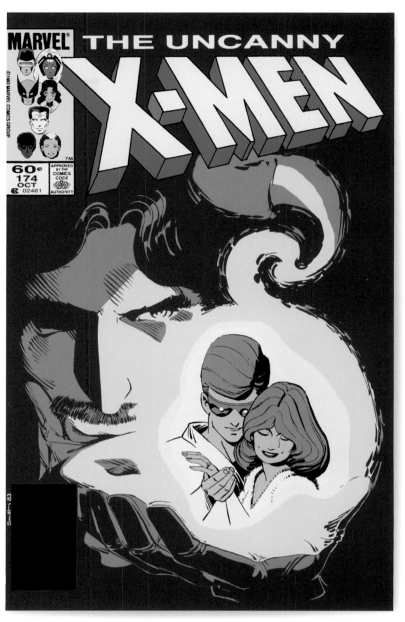

▲ *UNCANNY X-MEN* #168

April 1983
Artist: Paul Smith

Kitty Pryde was the standout star of Paul
Smith's run on *Uncanny X-Men*. This cover is
a compelling character study of Kitty, and the
story "Professor Xavier is a Jerk" was a favorite
of movie maker Joss Whedon, who later
referenced it during his stint as a writer on
Astonishing X-Men between 2004 and 2008.

▲ *UNCANNY X-MEN* #174

October 1983
Artist: Paul Smith

Paul Smith's penultimate cover on *Uncanny X-Men* is
a work of real beauty. It also harks back to the "Dark
Phoenix" saga, as it shows Mastermind watching
Cyclops and his new love Madelyne Pryor—who bore
an uncanny likeness to his dead wife Jean Grey. The
story had a real cliffhanger too, as Madelyne herself
apparently became the new Dark Phoenix.

◄ *UNCANNY X-MEN* #167

March 1983
Artist: Paul Smith

It took someone special to live up to the
high standards John Byrne had set on
Uncanny X-Men. Luckily artist Paul
Smith was more than able for the job,
and working with writer Chris Claremont,
they created a short run on the title that many
fans consider a series best. The cover for
this issue sees Cyclops holding Professor X's
corpse (an echo of the image on *X-Men* issue
#136). Professor X is not dead though—he has
just been taken over by the alien Brood.

December 1985
Artist: Arthur Adams

Arthur Adams burst onto the comic-book
scene illustrating *Longshot*. A true stylist,
Adams has always been famous for the
painstaking detail he puts into his art. His
work on the *Uncanny X-Men Annual* saw
Storm taken to Asgard to become the new
"Goddess of Thunder," her new Asgardian
look gracing the stunning cover.

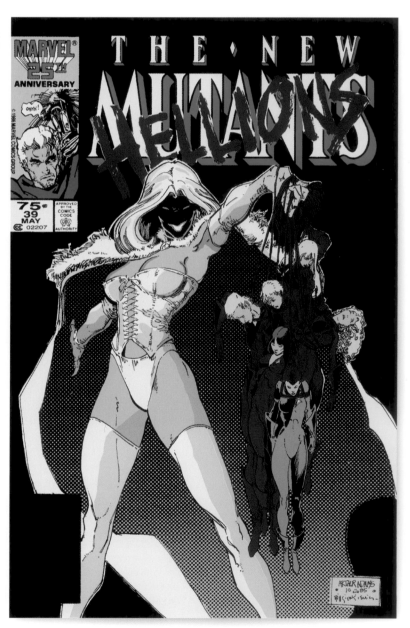

▲ *LONGSHOT #1*

September 1985
Artist: Arthur Adams

Adams' pencil work is exquisite and highly
detailed, and this cover was a stunning start by
the artist who quickly became one of the biggest
names in the business. *Longshot* was Adams'
first published work for Marvel. Written by Ann
Nocenti, issue #1 introduced a number of
characters—Longshot included—who would
eventually become part of the X-Men mythos.

▲ *THE NEW MUTANTS #39*

May 1986
Artist: Arthur Adams

Adams' work soon started gracing other covers,
too. His portrait of a villainous Emma Frost
holding up the corpses of the New Mutants is
particularly striking thanks to his detailed line
work. The story itself saw the New Mutants
become part of the Hellions at Emma Frost's
Massachusetts Academy—hence their name
spray painted over the title logo.

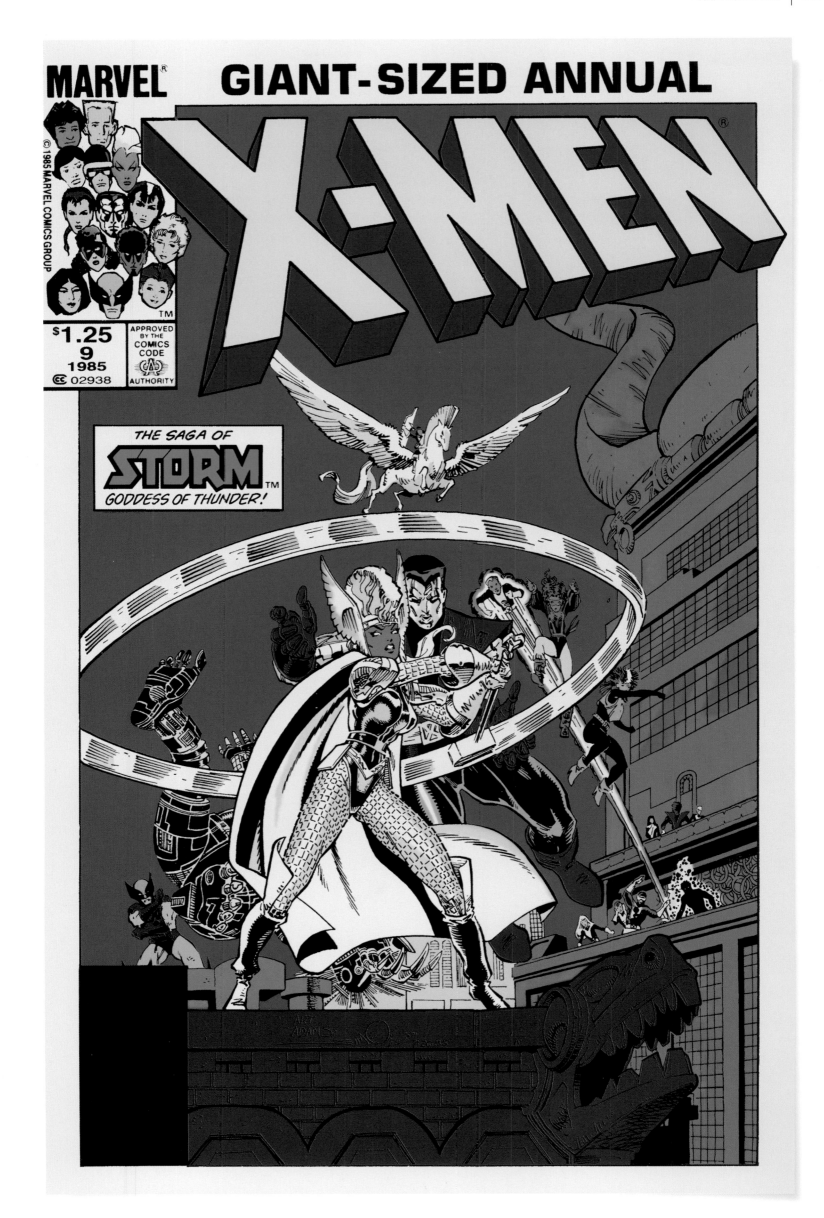

THE MODERN AGE

1986–

THE MID-1980s SAW a change in storytelling. Led by creators such as Alan Moore and Frank Miller, writers and artists started to explore darker, more adult themes in their comics. Alongside this, creator-owned comics came to the fore through the rise of publishers such as Image, Dark Horse, and Marvel's own Epic and Icon Imprints. This period also saw the rise of the X-Men. By the 1990s Marvel's mutants were not only a part of a best-selling comic, but also a huge franchise, with countless X-Men-related books in print.

A whole new generation of artists also burst onto the comic-book scene. Jim Lee, Marc Silvestri, Alan Davis, Carlos Pacheco, David Aja, and others started to push the boundaries of the art forward once again, creating some amazing covers along the way. By the 21st century, comics were becoming increasingly part of mainstream culture, with many top movies in Hollywood being based on Marvel heroes. The rise of digital publishing also gave readers a new way of reading comics. Publishing was changing, and Marvel was at the forefront of that change.

THE NEW AVENGERS #1 ▶

January 2005
Artist: David Finch

(Cover shown in full on p162)

▲ *AVENGERS* #1

February 1998
Artist: George Pérez

When *Avengers* was relaunched in 1998, Marvel put two of
its best at the helm—writer Kurt Busiek and artist George
Pérez. The latter produced a stunning cover for the debut
issue (shown here in full), featuring a host of potential
Avengers bursting out of the cover. Pérez had originally
made his name illustrating the title in the 1970s, but he
produced some of his best work on the new series.

AVENGERS #2 ▶

March 1998
Artist: George Pérez

George Pérez got to draw numerous
Avengers once again for the second
cover of the relaunched comic—but this
time with a twist. The evil Morgan le Fay
had altered reality into an Arthurian
world, transforming the heroes into
feudal versions of themselves. This
made for a very unusual cover image.

AVENGERS #503 ▶

December 2004
Artist: David Finch

David Finch produced a dark and thoughtful cover for the final part of the "Avengers Disassembled" epic, which saw the Avengers destroyed from within by an insane Scarlet Witch. The sight of Captain America surrounded by his friends' weaponry suggested that even more Avengers could die.

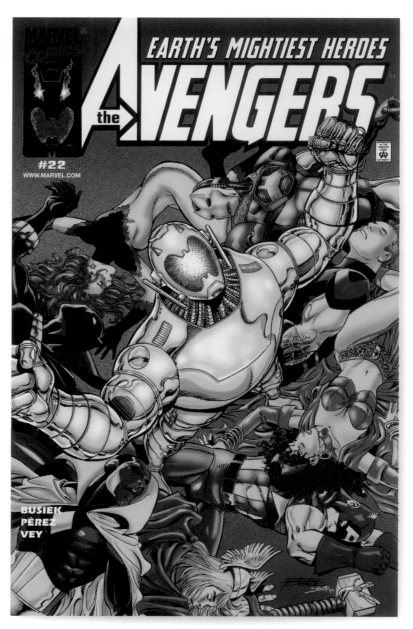

▲ *AVENGERS FOREVER* #1

December 1998
Artist: Carlos Pacheco

Avengers Forever was Kurt Busiek's complex, 12-part epic that brought together Avengers from across the timeline. The first issue's cover, by Carlos Pacheco, is a simple, but effective image featuring Rick Jones, the Hulk's old sidekick, contemplating a new line-up of the Avengers.

▲ *AVENGERS* #22

November 1999
Artist: George Pérez

Ultron, a robot created by Dr. Hank Pym in *Avengers* issue #55 (August 1968), has always been one of the team's deadliest enemies. This cover by George Pérez is one of the most menacing Ultron covers to date, showing the ferocious robot standing victorious over the defeated heroes.

AVENGERS FINALE

January 2005
Artist: Neal Adams

Legendary artist Neal Adams produced a stunning piece of work for the cover of the final *Avengers* comic (before the series was relaunched.) The dynamic nature of Adams' early work was back in full force with this image of the team charging into action. The story itself acted as an epilogue to the "Avengers Disassembled" storyline.

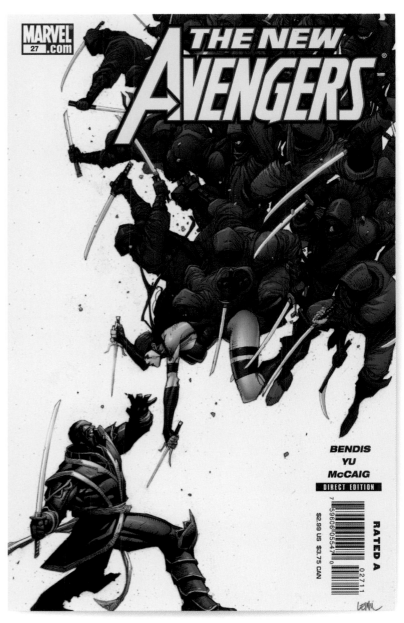

▲ *THE NEW AVENGERS* #2

February 2005
Artist: David Finch

With Spider-Man now a member of the Avengers, he soon became a regular on the covers. The second issue is another dramatic and tense-looking work from Finch. The image reflects the main story, as the heroes joined forces in an attempt to stop a mass breakout from the Super Villain penitentiary known as the Raft.

▲ *THE NEW AVENGERS* #27

April 2007
Artist: Leinil Francis Yu

Leinil Francis Yu produced this stylish cover during his brief run as artist on *The New Avengers*. His striking image shows new hero Ronin (Clint Barton taking over the role from Echo) facing off against an overwhelming horde of ninja assassins led by Elektra.

◄ *THE NEW AVENGERS* #1

January 2005
Artist: David Finch

This was the book that made the Avengers one of Marvel's bestsellers, and created an entire franchise, with various Avengers-related titles spinning off its success. The cover for issue #1 is darker and moodier than those of the previous title, and Finch instills a real sense of heroic power and mystery into the characters by showing them in half-shadow.

▲ *AVENGERS: THE INITIATIVE* #1

June 2007
Artist: Jim Cheung

Jim Cheung produced the art for a unique cover—or rather two covers—that could be put together to reveal one big image of the Avengers Initiative. Following on from the Civil War, which split Marvel's Super-Hero community in two, the new series focused on young heroes as they trained to be potential Avengers.

THE NEW AVENGERS: ILLUMINATI #1 ▶

February 2007
Artist: Jim Cheung

One of the most shocking revelations writer Brian Michael Bendis introduced to the Avengers was that six of Marvel's most respected heroes had formed a secret group—the Illuminati. Jim Cheung illustrated the series, his first cover bringing the heroes together in an atmospheric work that hints at the group's hidden affiliation.

▲ *AVENGERS CLASSIC* #1

August 2007
Artist: Art Adams

Art Adams created a stunning piece of work for the
debut issue of *Avengers Classic*, a series that reprinted
Avengers tales from their first issue (with some modern
material added). Adams manages to incorporate just
about every hero who had ever been an Avenger for his
cover. It was interesting to see Adams' artistic take on
the original team, including Iron Man, Thor, and the Hulk.

▲ *SECRET AVENGERS* #16

October 2011
Artist: John Cassaday

Famed writer Warren Ellis produced a tightly written series of one-shot stories for *Secret Avengers*, each graced with a cool, highly stylized cover by John Cassaday. In his first cover, Cassaday rotated his artwork from portrait to landscape, a radical move that perhaps reflected the strange time-travel story within.

▲ *SECRET AVENGERS* #17

November 2011
Artist: John Cassaday

John Cassaday surpassed himself with the next *Secret Avengers* cover. This relatively simple artwork shows Steve Rogers (during a spell where he wasn't Captain America), in front of an almost demonic-looking truck running him down. Using a limited color palette, Cassaday imbued the cover with a sense of danger and tension.

▲ *SECRET AVENGERS* #18

December 2011
Artist: John Cassaday

John Cassaday portrayed the martial-arts
hero Shang-Chi seemingly using his
skills to split someone's head in two on this
much-acclaimed cover. The shocking image
set the scene for another skilled Warren
Ellis story, with interior art by David Aja.

▲ *SECRET AVENGERS* #19

January 2012
Artist: John Cassaday

As Warren Ellis' run on *Secret Avengers* continued,
John Cassaday illustrated another stunning cover.
This time he placed the team in a cold, desolate
Eastern European landscape, their shadows
overlapping the logo, to highlight the covert
nature of the team. The story featured the
heroes taking down a gangster who was
using special drugs to increase his strength.

AVENGERS VS X-MEN #1 ▶

June 2012
Artist: Jim Cheung

When it was decided to pit the Avengers against the X-Men, Marvel knew they would need an A-list artist for this crossover event. Jim Cheung had broken into the world of comics as a teenager via Marvel UK and has gone on to become one of the industry's top artists. He provided the cover art for *Avengers vs. X-Men* (or *AVX*), showing both teams on the verge of war in a stunning piece of work.

◀ *AVENGERS* #1

July 2010
Artist: John Romita Jr.

The *Avengers* was relaunched following the end of the "Dark Reign," a period in Marvel continuity during which the unstable Norman Osborn gained political control of America's heroes. Steve Rogers, Osborn's more honorable successor, formed several new Avengers teams. Romita Jr.'s cover reflects the nobility of the main team and was the defining image of the new "Heroic Age."

◀ *UNCANNY AVENGERS* #1

December 2012
Artist: John Cassaday

Combining both the X-Men and Avengers into one team was a simple yet brilliant idea. John Cassaday, who had become one of the biggest names in the business by this time, illustrated the cover for the debut issue. Cassaday showcased the line-up and even incorporated the logo into his work, using it to separate the X-Men and Avengers.

◀ *CAPTAIN AMERICA ANNUAL* #8

September 1986
Artist: Mike Zeck

By the mid-1980s, Wolverine was firmly established as one of Marvel's favorite heroes, and an appearance by him on a cover would usually lead to an increase in sales. This was one of the most spectacular Wolverine covers outside of his own title. Mike Zeck's dynamic style gives the piece a dangerous energy fit for a Super Hero of Wolverine's standing.

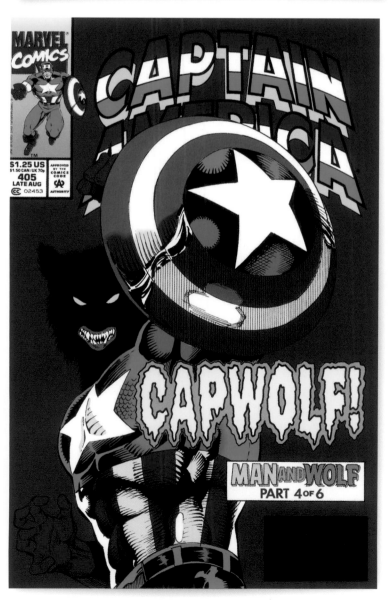

◀ *CAPTAIN AMERICA* #405

August 1992
Artist: Rik Levins

One of the strangest *Captain America* adventures saw Steve Rogers become a werewolf called "Capwolf." The Rik Levins cover has a simple layout, but the image of Capwolf is a striking and strangely intriguing one, typical of the title's experimental stories during the mid-90s.

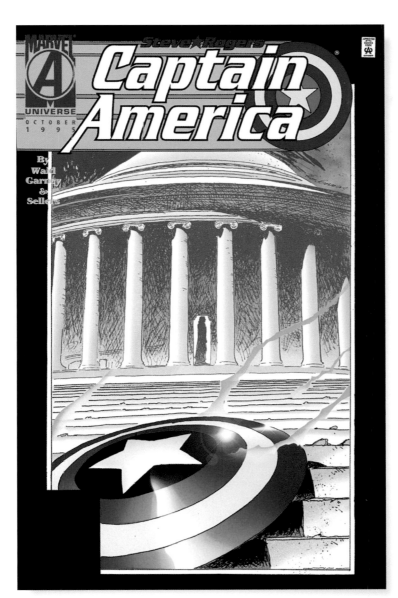

◀ *CAPTAIN AMERICA #444*

October 1995
Artist: Ron Garney

Writer Mark Waid and artist Ron Garney provided what many consider to be the best *Captain America* stories of the decade. Garney's covers were both stylish and eye-catching—and this one is a fine example. The discarded shield outside the White House hints at Cap's meeting with the President, and his eventual exile.

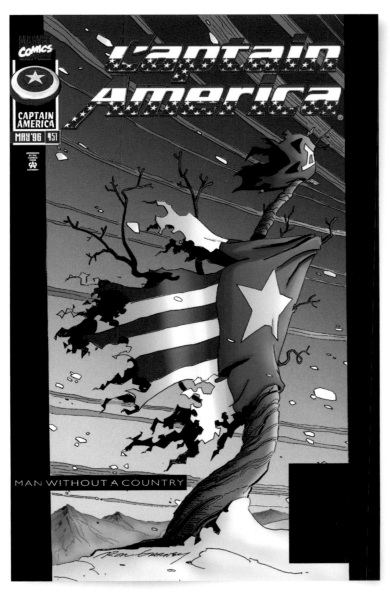

◀ *CAPTAIN AMERICA #451*

May 1996
Artist: Ron Garney

Ron Garney's stark cover reflected Steve Rogers taking up a new costume in this issue—one without the familiar stars and stripes emblazoned on it (seen here seemingly discarded and blowing in the wind). The striking image also obliquely refers to Cap's exile beyond US soil.

◀ *CAPTAIN AMERICA* #14

February 1999
Artist: Andy Kubert

Andy Kubert's terrifying portrait of the Red Skull made this Cap cover one of the most iconic of the decade. Writer Mark Waid's first run on *Captain America* had been cut short when the title was outsourced for a year to creators from publisher Image Comics. However, when the title returned, Marvel brought Waid back and relaunched the series from a new issue #1. It proved to be a huge success.

CAPTAIN AMERICA #32 ▶

August 2000
Artist: Andy Kubert

Andy Kubert got to draw Nick Fury and his Howling Commandos for this classic Captain America cover. Kubert's father, the legendary artist Joe Kubert, had made his name illustrating Sergeant Rock for DC Comics, and Andy's image has definite echoes of his father's work.

CAPTAIN AMERICA #1 ▶

June 2002
Artist: John Cassaday

The after-effects of the real-life 9/11 terrorist attacks that had taken place the previous year were felt in this issue as Cap was sent to the Middle East to find those responsible. Cassaday's stunning cover is über-patriotic and militaristic, reflecting a country—and indeed a world—trying to come to terms with the attacks.

▲ *CAPTAIN AMERICA* #1

January 2005
Artist: Steve Epting

Writer Ed Brubaker and artist Steve Epting created one of the all-time great *Captain America* sagas, "Out of Time." Epting's covers were exceptional montages, resembling high-end movie posters. This cover highlights a change in storytelling style, as Cap's adventures became more like a top-class spy-thriller than a traditional Super-Hero adventure.

▲ *CAPTAIN AMERICA* #6

June 2005
Artist: Steve Epting

Ed Brubaker's story gave a new twist to Bucky Barnes' role as Cap's old sidekick, making him a deadly assassin rather than teenage poster boy. Epting's cover for this issue focuses on Cap's exploits in World War II. It is another movie-style montage, the stark red Nazi flags providing a sinister backdrop.

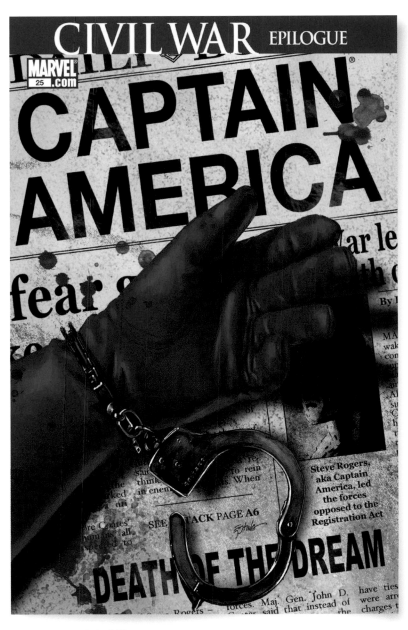

▲ *CAPTAIN AMERICA* #11

November 2005
Artist: Steve Epting

"The Winter Soldier" (Bucky Barnes, who had become a Soviet assassin since his days as Cap's sidekick) is the main focus on this issue's cover, with a montage of Bucky's war-time exploits behind him. The character and story was the inspiration for 2014's second *Captain America* movie.

▲ *CAPTAIN AMERICA* #25

April 2007
Artist: Ed McGuinness

Ed McGuinness' simple but emotionally charged cover illustrated a story that made headlines across the world—the assassination of Captain America. The headlines on the background image echo famous assassinations of real-life American heroes, making the cover all the more emotively powerful.

▲ INCREDIBLE HULK #333

July 1987
Artist: Steve Geiger

The Hulk had rarely looked as angry as he did on this cover, illustrated by Steve Geiger. Bruce Banner had just learned shocking secrets of his past. The trauma he felt was transferred to his monstrous alter ego, which Geiger brilliantly reflects in his depiction of a glowering Hulk.

▲ INCREDIBLE HULK #345

July 1988
Artist: Todd McFarlane

Todd McFarlane frequently reinvented (or simply broke) the rules of cover design in order to create an eye-catching image. This cover is a classic example—McFarlane made the logo part of the cover artwork, so he could have the gray, enraged Hulk smashing it up.

◄ INCREDIBLE HULK #340

February 1988
Artist: Todd McFarlane

Todd McFarlane's work on the Hulk (with writer Peter David) revitalized the hero and propelled McFarlane to the big league. This classic cover is a shining example of what made his run so popular. Since Wolverine's first appearance in *Incredible Hulk* issue #181 in November 1974 (after a cameo in issue #180), Hulk–Wolverine fights have always been a big deal. This artwork, with the gray Hulk cleverly reflected in Wolverine's claws, showcases one of the best.

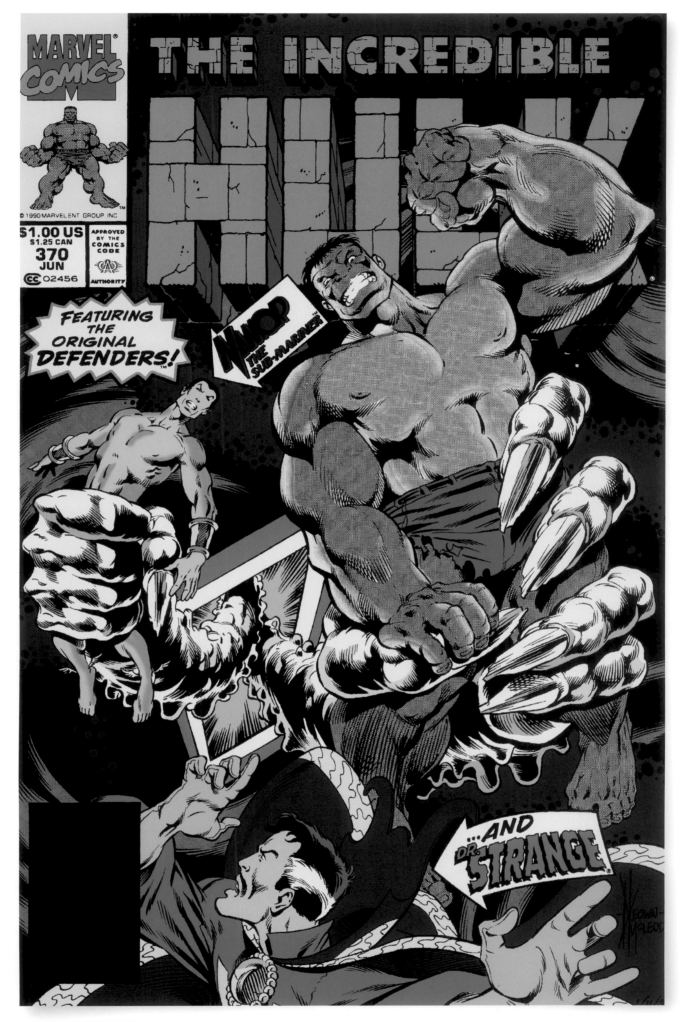

▲ *INCREDIBLE HULK #370*

June 1990
Artist: Dale Keown

Dale Keown followed Todd McFarlane as artist on *Incredible Hulk* and, working with writer Peter David, created what is considered by fans to be one of the title's best runs. Keown also produced a number of fantastic covers, including this one, which brings the original Defenders together for the first time in years.

▲ *INCREDIBLE HULK #373*

September 1990
Artist: Dale Keown

Peter David remains one of the best writers to chronicle the Hulk's adventures, bringing a sense of humanity to the character. This classic cover by Keown, featuring the Hulk and Betty Ross (Bruce Banner's main love interest) sharing a few laughs, best exemplifies that aspect of David and Keown's time on the title.

INCREDIBLE HULK **#379** ▶

March 1991
Artist: Dale Keown

One of the standout covers from Keown's run on *Incredible Hulk*, this issue marked the start of a new Hulk "persona," as Bruce Banner's intellect and the Hulk's physical form became one. The change was reflected in the title logo, which showed glimpses of previous incarnations of the Hulk. Keown's portrayal was about a mixture of power and intellect, the new Hulk managing to be both more human and more dangerous.

▲ *HULK* #11

April 2009
Artist: Ed McGuinness

Cover variants proved to be big news in the 2000s, and the second part of the "Defenders/Offenders War" story showed how alternative covers could be used to complement the main one. In this case the original cover shows the green Hulk and the Defenders while the variant shows the Red Hulk and the Offenders in a mirrored pose, providing a dramatic contrast between the two groups.

HULK & THING: HARD KNOCKS #1–4 ▶

November 2005–February 2006
Artist: Jae Lee

Artist Jae Lee created beautiful covers for this four-part series about the long rivalry between the Hulk and the Thing. The story, written by Bruce Jones, depicted the Hulk and the Thing talking over their old fights before coming to blows once again. Lee's close-up covers look like stills from the fight and also proved to be four of the most dramatic covers to feature the two heroes.

◄ *HAWKEYE* #1

October 2012
Artist: David Aja

Marvel's covers became increasingly stylized in the 2010s as artists pushed the boundaries of design. Writer Matt Fraction and artist David Aja produced one of the most adventurous Marvel comics in decades with *Hawkeye*. Each issue had a fabulous slick cover, and this debut issue set the standard for what was to follow. Aja eventually won a prestigious Eisner award for his work on this series.

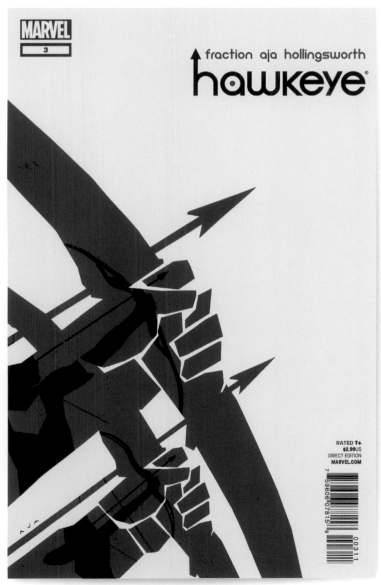

◄ *HAWKEYE* #3

December 2012
Artist: David Aja

David Aja's art, coupled with Matt Fraction's stories, led to the new *Hawkeye* series gaining rave reviews. Aja's third cover shows the weapons of two Hawkeyes—Clint Barton and Kate Bishop (Hawkeye of the *Young Avengers*). The image uses the same black, white, and purple color scheme of the early covers, which gave the book a distinctive look and set it apart from its competition.

◄ *HAWKEYE* #4

January 2013
Artist: David Aja

Issues #4 and #5 of *Hawkeye* are both fine examples of David Aja's stylistic and intelligent covers. The two-part story was called "The Tape" and involved Hawkeye trying to recover a politically sensitive video tape. The first part, in extreme contrast to most other Marvel Comics covers, simply shows a VHS cassette with sound waves below it, and lots of white space. It is enigmatic in its simplicity.

◄ *HAWKEYE* #5

February 2013
Artist: David Aja

The cover for the second part of "The Tape" was a dramatic and grisly contrast to that of part one. The blood splatters also signified the end of the "purple" cover phase. In a medium that usually employs action-packed, detailed covers, Aja's designs for *Hawkeye* were truly a breath of fresh air.

JOIN THE
R EVOLUTION

FRACTION
AJA
WU
HOLLINGSWORTH

008

HAWKEYE #9 ▶

May 2013
Artist: David Aja

This cover focuses on another Hawkeye, Kate Bishop. The young archer was becoming far more than a supporting character in the series, and this issue focused on her adventures rather than those of Clint Barton. Aja shows a keen sense for design on the cover, playing with both the logo and the brand to create a special cover image of Kate Bishop.

HAWKEYE #11 ▶

July 2013
Artist: David Aja

Pizza Dog takes center stage on the cover of one of the most inventive issues of *Hawkeye*. The image, showing the bloody pawprints left by Hawkeye's dog, reflects the fact that the whole issue is told from the dog's perspective. It was a unique cover for a unique series.

◀ *HAWKEYE* #8

April 2013
Artist: David Aja

While most comic-book covers often utilize bright visuals, few use one color in such a dominant way as this "Valentine special" issue of *Hawkeye*. The central image of Cherry (one of Clint Barton's many ex-girlfriends) on a blood-red background really conveys a feeling of violence and danger. With such bold use of color and imagery, artist David Aja pushed the boundaries of design in ways not seen since the days of Jim Steranko.

IRON MAN #1

February 1998
Artist: Sean Chen

Sean Chen became the regular artist for *Iron Man* when the title reemerged with the "Heroes Return" stories. Chen's cover for the first issue showcases the Armored Avenger in a new version of his classic red-and-gold costume. It promised a fresh and exciting take on the character.

▲ *INVINCIBLE IRON MAN #20*

January 2010
Artist: Salvador Larroca

This slightly surreal cover perfectly captured a turning point in the life of Tony Stark and Iron Man as the hero struggled to reboot his mind after he had wiped it to stop Norman Osborn from learning his secrets. All five parts of this storyline reflected Stark's inner struggle. This first part showcased Stark's concern that he would never regain his lost knowledge.

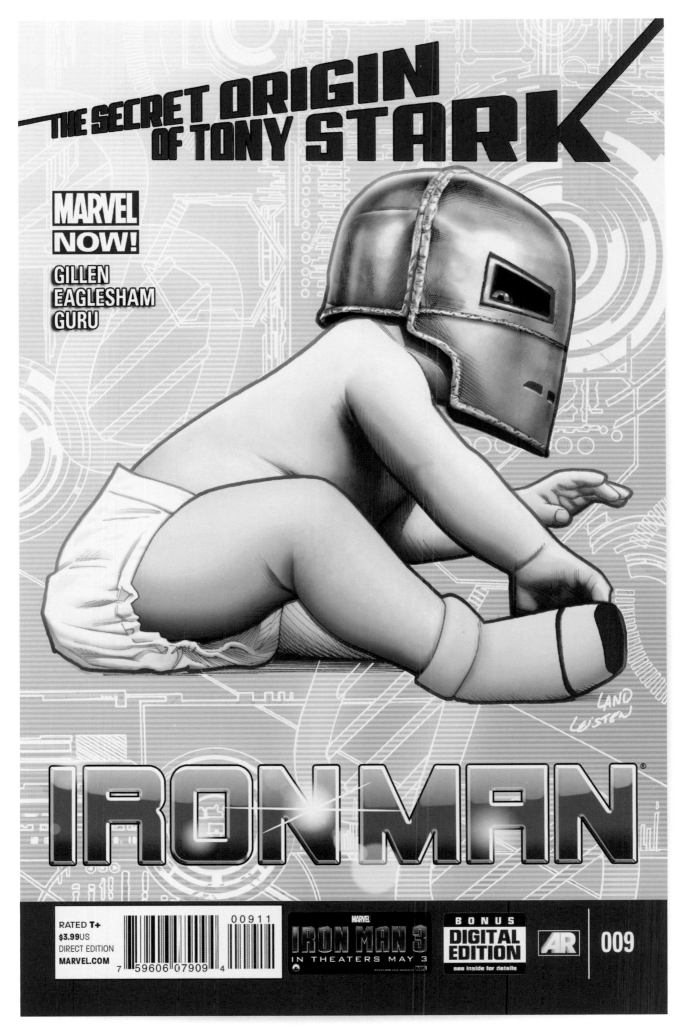

▲ *IRON MAN #9*

June 2013
Artist: Greg Land

Few covers can claim to be truly original, but this Greg
Land piece, showing an infant Tony Stark, managed it.
It signalled the start of one of the most shocking *Iron
Man* stories of all time, as writer Kieron Gillen's story
seemed to suggest alien intervention leading up to
Stark's birth—only to reveal that Tony had been adopted
and that the Stark's natural son Arno, was still alive.

▲ *THOR* #1

July 1998
Artist: John Romita Jr.

When Thor's own series was relaunched
following the end of the "Heroes Reborn"
saga, John Romita Jr. was brought in as
the artist. His powerful style was the
perfect match for Thor, who has rarely
looked as godlike as he does on this
stunning wraparound cover.

THOR #1 ▶

September 2007
Artist: Olivier Coipel

The first new *Thor* comic since
2004 needed to feature something
special on the cover. Artist Olivier
Coipel's interpretation of the
powerful God of Thunder shows
a new, darker look for Thor than
had been seen previously.

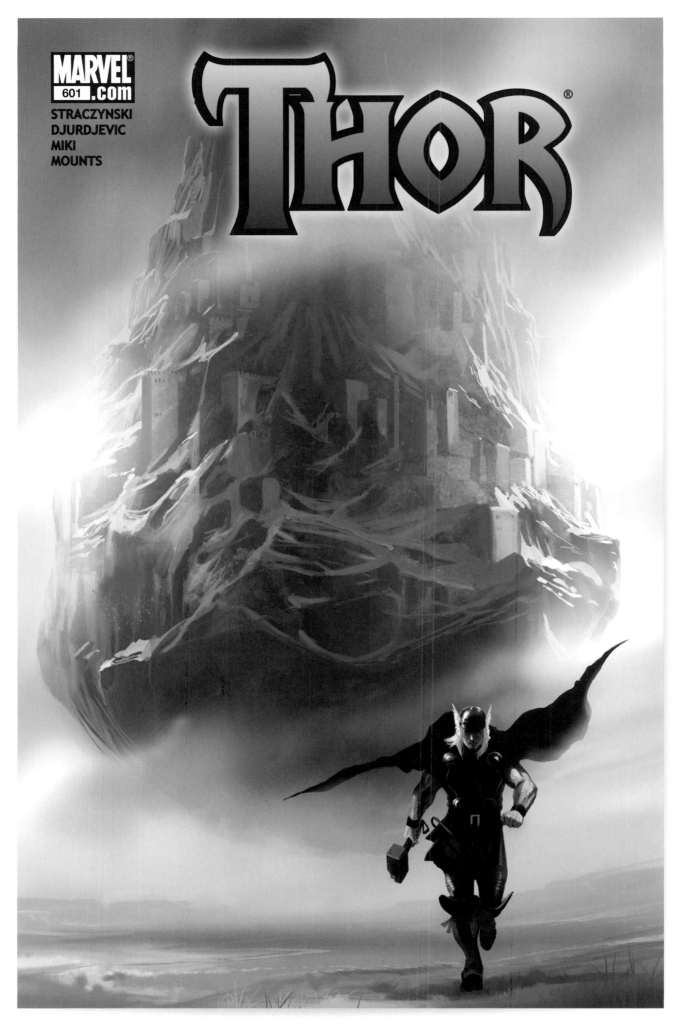

▲ *THOR* #601

June 2009
Artist: Marko Djurdjevic

This issue boasts one of the most beautiful covers in *Thor*'s history, and one of the greatest modern interpretations of Thor's home, Asgard. Marko Djurdjevic captured Thor's anger and melancholy at being exiled from Asgard in one moody, expressionistic piece. This art style had a big influence on the first *Thor* movie (2011).

▲ *LOKI* #1

September 2004
Artist: Esad Ribic

Thor's evil adopted brother, Loki, gained his
very own miniseries, with Esad Ribic creating
beautifully painted covers for all four issues.
Each one showcased Loki's troubled relationship
with the Thunder God. The first, showing Loki
looming menacingly over his captured brother,
set the scene for the Loki-centric series.

▲ *JOURNEY INTO MYSTERY* #625

September 2011
Artist: Stephanie Hans

Stephanie Hans' romantic-looking cover belies
writer Kieron Gillen's dark and ultimately tragic
fantasy told within. Far from being a romantic
tale, issue #625 told the story of a young Loki
attempting to save the world from the Serpent,
an ancient Asgardian God of Fear.

◀ *THOR: AGES OF THUNDER* #1

June 2008
Artist: Marko Djurdjevic

Thor: Ages of Thunder recounted
tales of Thor's Asgardian adventures.
Artist Marko Djurdjevic created a
suitably mythic-looking cover for this
one-off issue, showing the Thunder God
standing triumphantly on a defeated Frost
Giant. Other one-shots, telling more tales
of Thor's Asgardian life, soon followed,
each with a highly detailed Djurdjevic cover.

FANTASTIC FOUR #348 ▶

January 1991
Artist: Art Adams

This issue's cover (and the story inside) brought together four of Marvel's most popular heroes of the time—Ghost Rider, the Hulk, Spider-Man, and Wolverine—into an all-new *Fantastic Four*. Add artist Art Adams producing some of his finest work, and you have a classic *Fantastic Four* cover. The heroes joined forces to rescue the original team, who had been captured by a rogue Skrull.

◀ **FANTASTIC FOUR #345**

October 1990
Artist: Walt Simonson

Could the Fantastic Four really be dead? That was the question raised by the image of a triceratops with torn FF costumes hanging out of its mouth. The strapline was changed from the usual "World's Greatest Comic Magazine" to "Prehistory's Greatest Comic Magazine" to reflect the time-travel nature of the story as Simonson's inventive run on the title continued.

◀ **FANTASTIC FOUR #349**

February 1991
Artist: Art Adams

Art Adams produced another outstanding piece of work for this cover, lining the original Fantastic Four up alongside a new team that had formed to save them following their capture in the previous issue. The sight of all the heroes together, alongside the Mole Man, marching out towards the reader resulted in an eye-catching cover.

◄ *FANTASTIC FOUR #60*

October 2002
Artist: Mike Wieringo

Mike Wieringo's cover art for the *Fantastic Four* conveyed a sense of wonder that only the best FF artists brought to the title, while Mark Waid's scripts ensured a series of great stories. Such was Marvel's confidence in this new creative duo that they released the issue for only 9 cents.

◄ *FANTASTIC FOUR #61*

November 2002
Artist: Mike Wieringo

The Thing was perhaps the most human of Marvel's monstrous heroes, and artist Mike Wieringo's interpretation manages to encapsulate this theme perfectly. He evokes not only The Thing's amazing strength, but also his inner nobility.

◄ *FANTASTIC FOUR #67*

May 2003
Artist: Mike Wieringo

This issue was a prologue to "Unthinkable," a highlight of Mark Waid and Mike Wieringo's time working on the *Fantastic Four*. Wieringo's striking cover portrays a powerful and despotic Doctor Doom burning with energy gained through selling the soul of his true love to demons.

◄ *FANTASTIC FOUR #558*

August 2008
Artist: Bryan Hitch

Doctor Doom has been the subject of many great covers, but Bryan Hitch's startling close-up of Latveria's dictator presented a new aspect to the character. It is one of the only times Doom has looked scared on a cover, making the reader instantly want to find out exactly what, or who, Doom feared so much.

◀ *FANTASTIC FOUR 1234* **#1**

October 2001
Artist: Jae Lee

Working with writer Grant Morrison, Jae Lee brought his unique vision to the Fantastic Four on a four-part miniseries, which focused on the bonds that united the team. Lee's illustration of Yancy Street, once home to Ben Grimm, established the dark, moody tone of the series. As Ben desperately tried to alter his own past so that he never became the Thing, evil Doctor Doom was masterminding the team's destruction.

FF **#12** ▶

January 2012
Artist: Steve Epting

The FF—or Future Foundation—replaced the Fantastic Four both as a team and a comic in the 2010s. The FF was actually an organization for young, gifted minds, founded by Mr. Fantastic. Epting's simple cover shines the spotlight on these great young characters (and a reformed, intelligent Dragon Man), and brought a fresh energy to the book.

FF **#6** ▶

June 2013
Artist: Mike Allred

The FF gained a second volume, written by Matt Fraction and illustrated by Mike Allred. The new series was strange, funny, and sometimes bizarre—as exemplified by this crazy cover showing new FF member Darla Deering (aka Miss Thing) being stalked by a masked Yancy Street Gang, who resented her taking on the role of the Thing.

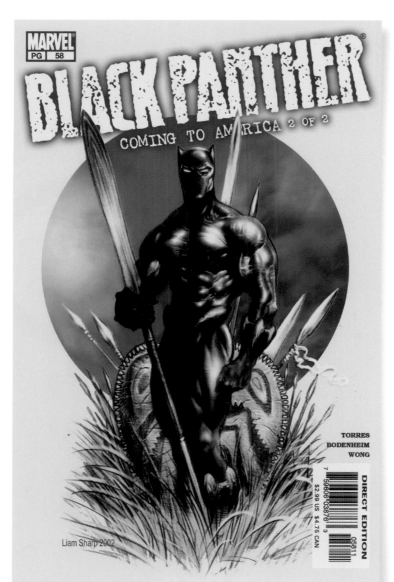

◀ BLACK PANTHER #58

June 2003
Artist: Liam Sharp

The Black Panther was one of Marvel's first African heroes and Liam Sharp used the Panther's African background to add some beautiful design elements to his cover. The bright African sun helps to frame the Panther and gives the image an almost mythical element.

BLACK PANTHER #11 ▶

February 2006
Artist: Mike Deodato Jr.

Comic fans always love team-ups and this issue had one of the coolest. Black Panther joined forces with the Falcon, Shang Chi, and Luke Cage to take on Shang Chi's estranged father Han (a criminal mastermind). Deodato's cover brought all the main players together in one stylish image that also reflected the villain's Asian powerbase.

◀ BLACK PANTHER:
THE MOST DANGEROUS MAN ALIVE #525

January 2012
Artist: Francesco Francavilla

When Black Panther took over Daredevil's title from issue #513, the new series produced a number of adventurous cover designs. The covers that Francavilla produced for "The Most Dangerous Man Alive" story-arc had a real pulp-fiction detective-story look, right down to the faded colors. The cover featured the Panther's latest adversary, the Kingpin.

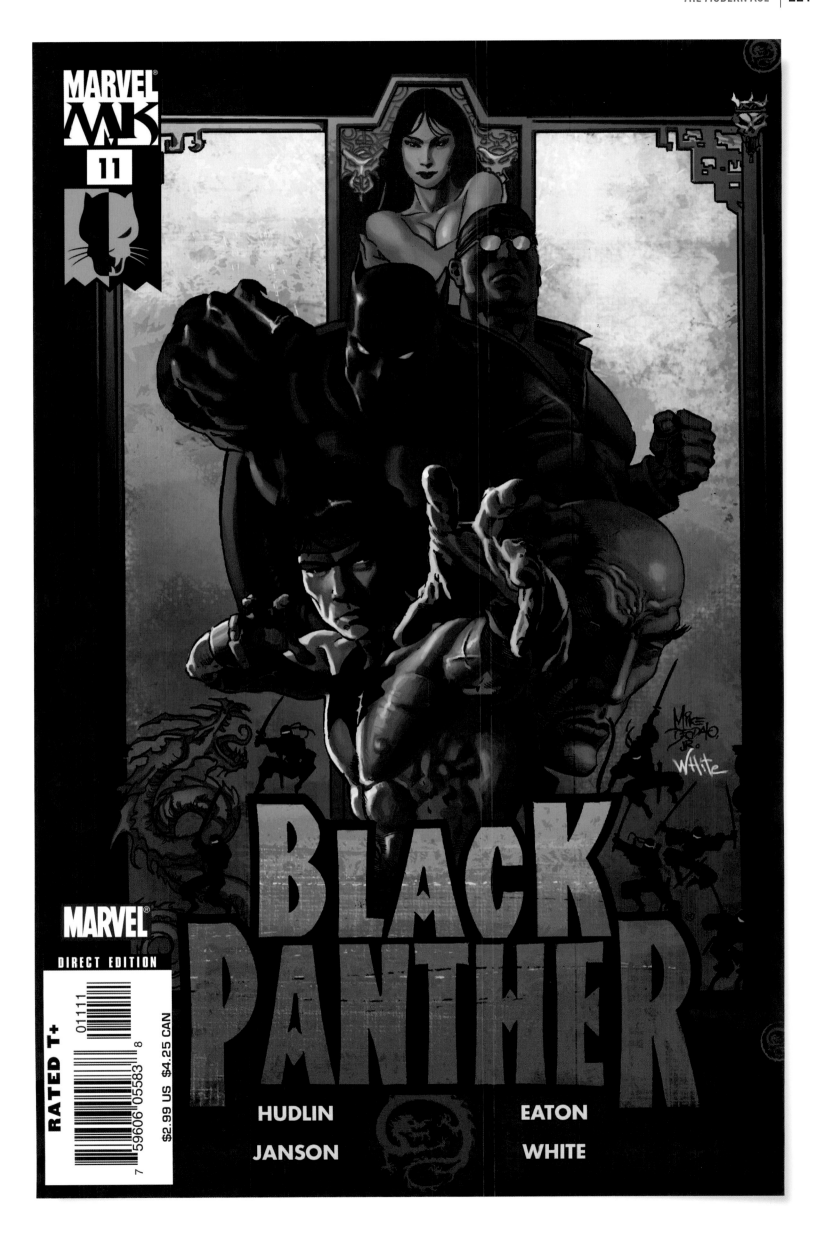

BLACK PANTHER #1

April 2005

Artist: John Romita Jr.

For the creation of the *Black Panther* issue #1 cover, John Romita Jr. started the process the traditional way, creating a number of rough character poses (1) before moving onto pencils. Once these were approved, the finished pencils (2) were inked by the legendary Klaus Janson (3) before passing on to Dean White for coloring (4). White colored the cover on computer, but gave it a natural, painterly feel to reflect the subject of the piece. The finished art was then sent digitally to Marvel, whose design team added the Marvel branding, before turning the cover into a high-resolution format ready for print (5). With the advent of direct sales to comic shops, covers are now produced months in advance of the final comic-book art, so that they can be used for advanced promotion.

1. Sketch
2. Pencil
3. Ink
4. Color
5. Final cover

1.

2.

3.

4.

INHUMANS #1 ▶

November 1998
Artist: Jae Lee

The cover of the first issue of this 12-part series is a powerful one. It portrays the Inhuman royal family with their king, Black Bolt, in the forefront, flanked by his wife Medusa and his closest allies. The Inhumans look both regal and alien, thanks to Lee's dark and stylish work.

INHUMAN #1 ▶

April 2014
Artist: Joe Madureira

Top artist Joe Madureira returned to Marvel to illustrate Inhuman. The cover shows the Inhumans covertly living side-by-side with humanity. They were Inhumans who—like the title's hero, Dante – had no knowledge of their true genetic origins until exposure to the Inhumans' Terrigen Mists brought out their Inhuman abilities. This issue marks the increased importance of the Inhumans in the wider Marvel Universe.

◀ THE INHUMANS #1-4

June–October 2000
Artist: José Ladrönn

The third volume of The Inhumans was a four-part miniseries, written by Rafael Marin and illustrated by José Ladrönn. Each cover reflects the alien nature of the Inhumans' origins, a focal point of the series, with a close-up of one or two of the main Inhumans—Black Bolt, Medusa, and Karnak and Triton. Issue #4 featured the Inhumans' enemy Ronan the Accuser.

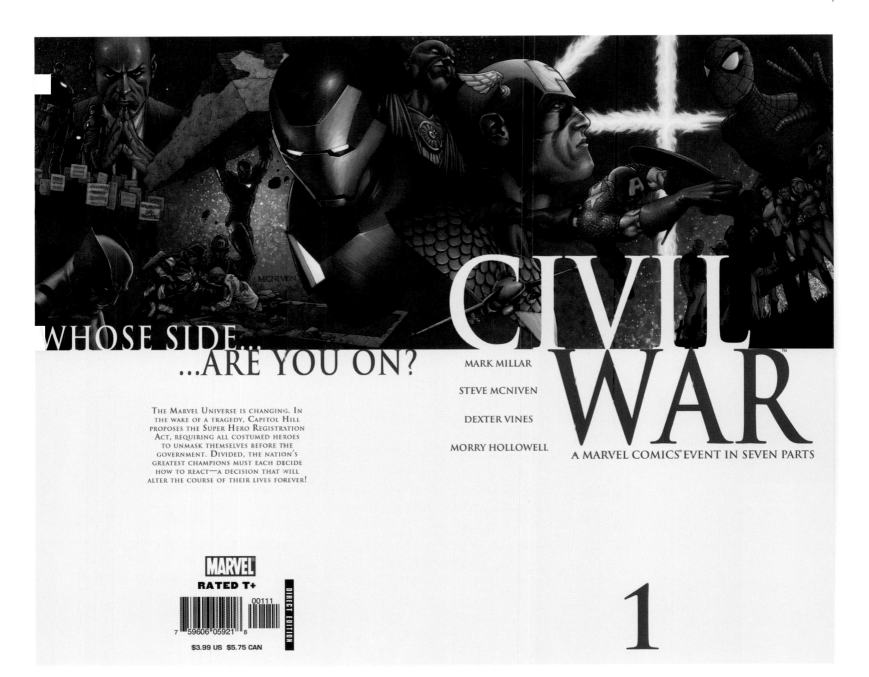

WHOSE SIDE...
...ARE YOU ON?

THE MARVEL UNIVERSE IS CHANGING. IN THE WAKE OF A TRAGEDY, CAPITOL HILL PROPOSES THE SUPER HERO REGISTRATION ACT, REQUIRING ALL COSTUMED HEROES TO UNMASK THEMSELVES BEFORE THE GOVERNMENT. DIVIDED, THE NATION'S GREATEST CHAMPIONS MUST EACH DECIDE HOW TO REACT—A DECISION THAT WILL ALTER THE COURSE OF THEIR LIVES FOREVER!

CIVIL WAR

MARK MILLAR

STEVE MCNIVEN

DEXTER VINES

MORRY HOLLOWELL

A MARVEL COMICS EVENT IN SEVEN PARTS

MARVEL
RATED T+
DIRECT EDITION
7 59606 05921 8
00111
$3.99 US $5.75 CAN

1

CIVIL WAR #1 ▲

July 2006
Artist: Steve McNiven

Marvel created a new design style for the launch of *Civil War*, the company's 2006 saga that made headlines across the world. Steve McNiven's striking cover for the first issue hints at the drama to come, while the white border and careful placement of text revealed the increasing role that design was playing in Marvel's covers as they sought new ways to make their comics stand out.

◄ *THE INFINITY GAUNTLET* #1

July 1991
Artist: George Pérez

Award-winning artist George Pérez was at the helm for *The Infinity Gauntlet*, one of Marvel's first comic-book blockbusters. Pérez's stunning cover for the first issue displays a host of Marvel's Super Heroes around the central image of Thanos. The cover established the star-spanning nature of the series, with heroes such as Silver Surfer and the Hulk caught up in Thanos' attempt to impress Death by wiping out half of the universe.

◄ ANNIHILATION: CONQUEST—STARLORD #1

September 2007
Artist: Nic Klein

The success of *Annihilation* led to a follow-up, *Annihilation: Conquest*, which saw Marvel's cosmic heroes facing a new threat—the Phalanx. The series had started with a prologue that led into several miniseries, including one featuring Starlord. Artist Nic Klein created an action-packed pose for the first cover, depicting the hero blasting his guns out at the reader.

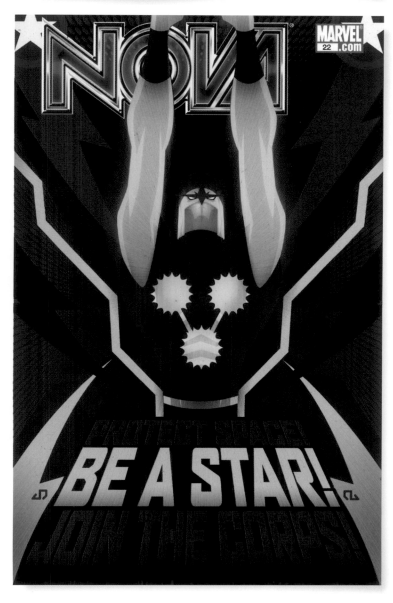

◄ NOVA #22

April 2009
Artist: Juan Doe

Writers Andy Lanning and Dan Abnett re-established *Nova* as one of Marvel's greatest cosmic heroes and—by this issue—left the hero close to death after his powers had been stripped from him by the alien entity Worldmind. This issue heralded the return of the Nova Corps, with Juan Doe turning the cover into a stylish recruitment poster for the new corps.

◀ *ANNIHILATION: CONQUEST* #5

May 2008
Artist: Aleksi Briclot

As *Annihilation: Conquest* continued its run, this cover revealed the true bad guy of the series—leader of the Phalanx, Ultron. Aleksi Briclot's image of the Avengers' old enemy sitting astride a throne was one of the most powerful interpretations of the villain. The series also featured the characters who would become the new Guardians of the Galaxy.

◀ *ANNIHILATION: CONQUEST* #6

June 2008
Artist: Aleksi Briclot

Some of Marvel's greatest cosmic heroes appeared together for this final part of *Annihilation: Conquest*. Briclot's cover, with its dramatic use of color and lighting, gives the reader the sense that the heroes, led by Adam Warlock, are about to face their greatest battle yet against Ultron and the Phalanx.

GUARDIANS OF THE GALAXY #7 ▶

November 2013
Artist: Sara Pichelli

Artist Sara Pichelli perfectly captured the chaotic swagger and the bold attitude of the new group of guardians on this cover. The illustration shows the mismatched heroes in an art style that set the group apart from existing teams of Super Heroes.

◀ *GUARDIANS OF THE GALAXY* #1

July 2008
Artist: Clint Langley

Andy Lanning and Dan Abnett masterminded a modern-day relaunch for *Guardians of the Galaxy*. The new guardians were a disparate group of alien heroes. Chris Langley's cover quickly established the fast-paced style of the new series, and created a look that would carry the team to the big screen in 2014.

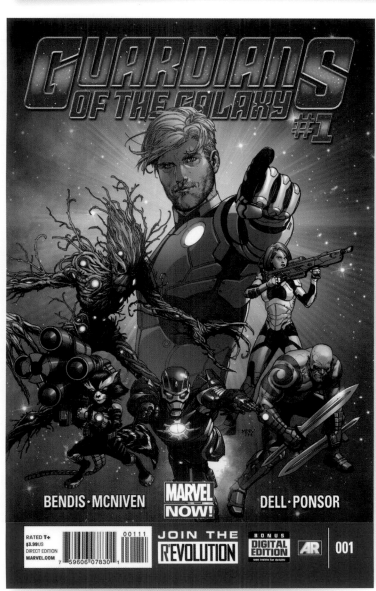

◀ *GUARDIANS OF THE GALAXY* #1

May 2013
Artist: Steve McNiven

Guardians of the Galaxy was relaunched again as part of 2013's Marvel Now! branding. Artist Steve McNiven used a team shot on the cover to introduce the heroes, featuring Star-Lord front and center. This new series boosted the groups' standing in the Marvel Universe to coincide with the release of the *Guardians of the Galaxy* movie in 2014.

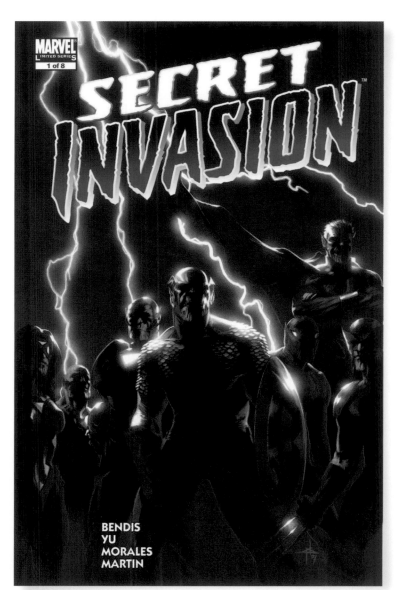

◄ *SECRET INVASION* #1

June 2008
Artist: Gabriele Dell'Otto

Marvel's big event of 2008 saw Earth invaded by shape-changing Skrulls. Gabriele Dell'Otto's cover for the first issue depicts humanity's greatest heroes in shadow, the Skrull outlines of their faces just visible. It was a clear message that no hero could be trusted and, as far as this storyline was concerned, anyone could be a Skrull.

◄ *MS. MARVEL* #25

May 2008
Artist: Greg Horn

The Skrull "Secret Invasion" spread beyond the central series, with various Marvel titles featuring Skrull-themed covers. Greg Horn's painting of a Skrull Ms. Marvel hints that the title's lead character might be an alien—a fact that was central to the storyline as those closest to the heroine started to doubt her.

◄ *MIGHTY AVENGERS* #15

August 2008
Artist: Marko Djurdjevic

As the "Secret Invasion" continued,
some heroes found out that they
had been Skrulls all along—and in
some cases, never even realized it.
One of the biggest shocks was the
revelation that Yellowjacket was
a Skrull. Djurdjevic's cover shows
that not only was Yellowjacket a
Skrull, but he was one who had
started to enjoy his life as an Avenger
too much and was replaced by his
Skrull masters. It also acted as a
homage to *Avengers* issue #213
(November 1981), in terms of the
layout and character poses.

◄ *GUARDIANS OF THE GALAXY* #4

October 2008
Artist: Clint Langley

The "Secret Invasion" of Earth
was now in full force and soon even
Marvel's star-spanning heroes were
affected by it. Covers such as this
one, by artist Clint Langley, helped
to convey one of the main ideas of
"Secret Invasion"—that behind
their masks any hero could be a
Skrull, even an interplanetary one
such as Star-Lord.

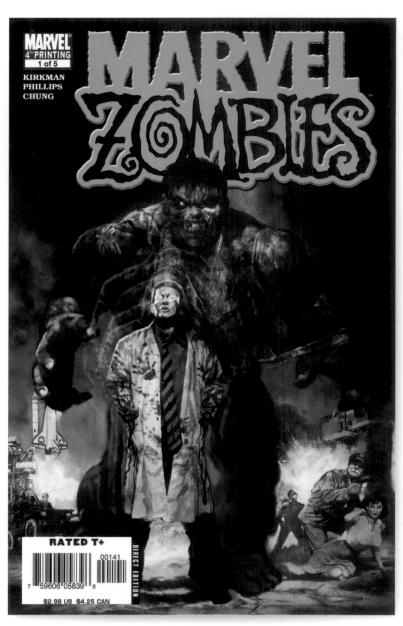

▲ *MARVEL ZOMBIES* #1

February 2006
Artist: Arthur Suydam

Arthur Suydam's zombified paintings of classic
Marvel covers were a big reason for the success of
Marvel Zombies (a title written by *The Walking Dead*
creator Robert Kirkman). The original cover of the
first issue in the series was a homage to *Amazing
Fantasy* issue #15 (August 1962; *see p50*) and the
first appearance of Spider-Man.

▲ *MARVEL ZOMBIES* #1 (FOURTH PRINTING VARIANT)

April 2006
Artist: Arthur Suydam

Cover variants became increasingly popular in the
2000s, with avid collectors seeking out every version
of a cover. This fourth printing of *Marvel Zombies*
issue #1 featured a homage to *Incredible Hulk* issue
#1 (May 1962; *see p28*). A zombie Hulk was one of
the standout characters of the series, his stomach
bloated with the friends he had eaten.

▲ *MARVEL ZOMBIES #3*

April 2006
Artist: Arthur Suydam

This *Marvel Zombies* cover was another homage, this time to Todd McFarlane's classic *Incredible Hu'k* issue #340 (February 1988; *see p178*). Additions such as the bloody eyeballs in Wolverine's mouth conveyed the setting of this story—a world filled with zombie Super Heroes—and are also what made Suydam's work so very eye-catching.

▲ *MARVEL ZOMBIES #4*

May 2006
Artist: Arthur Suydam

This homage to *The X-Men* issue #1 (September 1963; *see p60*)—with a grisly Cyclops holding his own severed head in his arms and Beast's arms falling off—is a perfect example of the humor that made *Marvel Zombies* a smash hit. Suydam's zombies lived on long after the series, appearing as variants on many other Marvel titles.

◀ DAREDEVIL #227

February 1986
Artist: David Mazzucchelli

After a three-year absence, comic-book megastar Frank Miller returned to *Daredevil* as a writer to mastermind one of the hero's greatest stories. Known as "Born Again," the story arc saw the Kingpin learn Daredevil's secret identity, and then set out to ruin him. David Mazzucchelli produced stunning art for both the cover and the story.

◀ DAREDEVIL #228

March 1986
Artist: David Mazzucchelli

Each cover of the "Born Again" saga had a religiously themed tagline. "Purgatory" was the perfect summation of Daredevil's suffering in this dark issue. The cover image reflects the chaotic, terrified state of Matt Murdock's mind, the cracks revealing how close to insanity the hero is as a result of the Kingpin tearing apart his life.

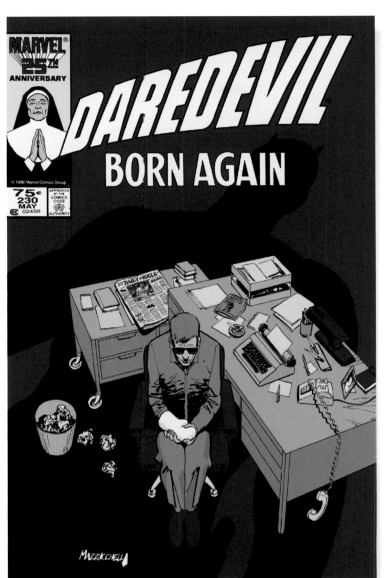

◀ *DAREDEVIL #230*

May 1986
Artist: David Mazzucchelli

This key issue in the "Born Again" saga featured reporter Ben Urich on the cover. Daredevil's shadow looms over Urich as he tries to come to terms with death threats caused by his connection to the hero. The saga saw most of the main characters going through their own personal hells to be born again as better people.

◀ *DAREDEVIL #232*

July 1986
Artist: David Mazzucchelli

Mazzucchelli's penultimate cover for the "Born Again" saga saw the debut of Nuke, a villainous product of the secret Super Soldier program that had created Captain America. As Nuke's tattooed face peers over at Daredevil on the cover, the story's religious themes were given a military twist in the cover line, "God and Country."

1.

2.

3.

JOHN ROMITA JR.

John Romita Jr. has been one of Marvel's top artists for over 40 years. From producing pages for Marvel UK as a young man, to his more recent work on Marvel's leading titles, John Romita Jr. has drawn just about every Marvel character going. While at first his art echoed the clean, commercial style of his father, Romita's art evolved during his run on *Daredevil* (1988–1990), becoming more confident, powerful, and increasingly filled with energy. It was a style that propelled him to the very top of his field. As art legend Joe Kubert said, "His style is one immediately recognizable, and the movement combined with impact and clarity of his storytelling is what cartooning is all about."

1. *WOLVERINE* #20
December 2004

This early sketch of Wolverine saw John Romita Jr. experiment with a different angle for the hero compared to the one finally used *(see p296)*. His loose pencil style still shows the raw power of his finished work.

2. *AMAZING SPIDER-MAN* #43
September 2002

Romita Jr. enjoyed two successful runs on *Amazing Spider-Man* and this cover exemplifies what made his second spell on the title so popular. It is a brooding, atmospheric work, perfectly bringing out the arachnid in Spider-Man, who was perched behind a ledge as a storm raged behind him.

3. *UNCANNY X-MEN* #207
July 1986

This cover showcases the dynamism of Romita's art during his first run on *Uncanny X-Men*. It also shows his use of inventive design and layout skills as Wolverine's claws tear dramatically through the cover.

4. *DAREDEVIL: THE MAN WITHOUT FEAR* #1
October 1993

Romita Jr. himself considers his work with Frank Miller on this title to be some of his best. This cover shows the highly detailed line-work Romita had developed during this period, as well as his ability to convey raw emotion and drama in his art.

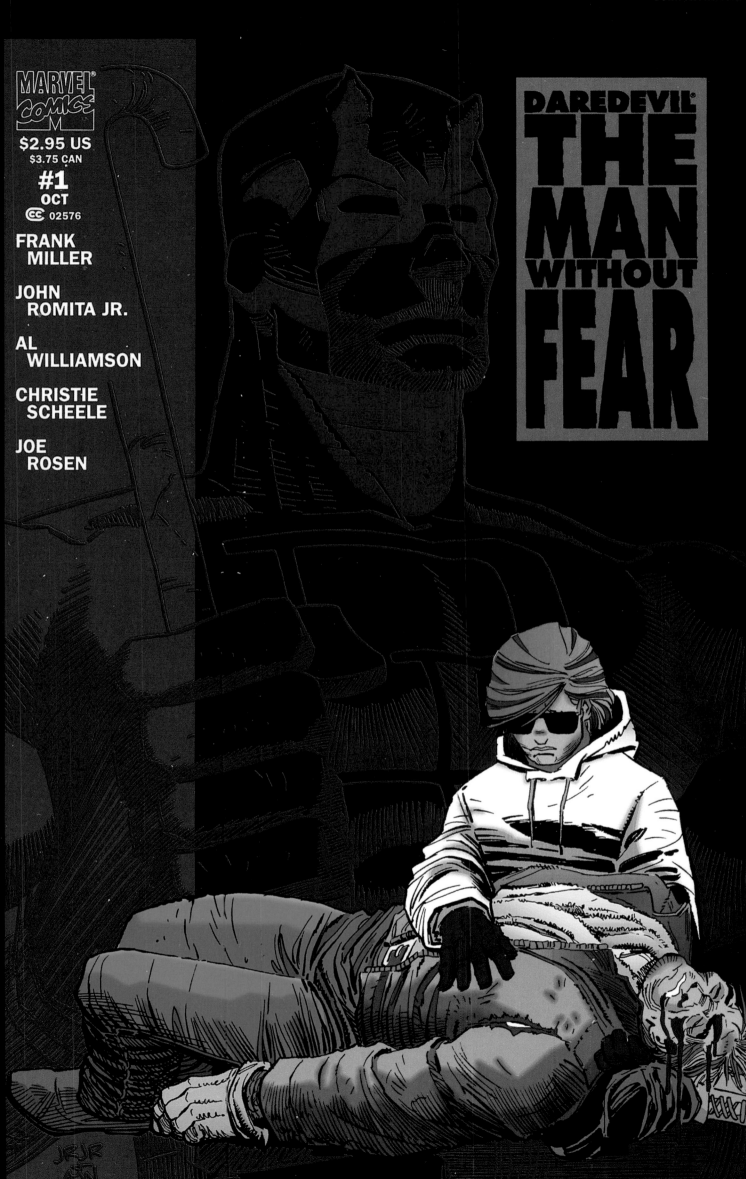

MARVEL KNIGHTS #1 ▶

July 2000
Artist: Joe Quesada

The Marvel Knights imprint gained a team book with this issue, which brought together Shang Chi, Punisher, Dagger, Daredevil, and the Black Widow. The team had a more urban feel than other groups, and although they weren't officially a team, the heroes fought together against a number of foes. Joe Quesada illustrated the cover to the first issue and used the rope of Daredevil's Billy Club to add a sense of movement and energy to the atmospheric image.

▲ *DAREDEVIL #3*

January 1999
Artist: Joe Quesada

This atmospheric Joe Quesada cover captures the story's religious elements. Matt Murdock's Catholicism had often played a major part in the comic's storylines. His beliefs were once again laid bare as the hero tried to protect a young baby he would soon come to believe could be the Messiah—or the Antichrist.

▲ *DAREDEVIL #8*

June 1999
Artist: Joe Quesada

Smith and Quesada's "Guardian Devil" epic came to a close this issue, which acted as an epilogue to the main saga. Quesada's cover, showing Spider-Man and Daredevil, was a calm change of pace after the tension and shocks of the previous issues. It reflects the melancholy nature of the climax, as Matt mourned Karen Page.

◀ *DAREDEVIL* #32

June 2002
Artist: Alex Maleev

Writer Brian Michael Bendis and artist Alex Maleev had a long and award-winning run on *Daredevil*, creating several twists along the way. This issue's cover reflects one of the biggest twists—the FBI started to suspect that Matt Murdock was Daredevil. Maleev had a fine arts background and his covers were often experimental, blending drawing with digital and photorealistic techniques.

◀ *DAREDEVIL* #46

June 2003
Artist: Alex Maleev

Typhoid Mary, one of Daredevil's deadliest and most complex foes, returned in this issue, with Alex Maleev providing a sensual new interpretation of the villain for the cover. Bendis and Maleev managed to create a series of stories that broke new ground for the Man Without Fear—without turning their backs on the character's rich history.

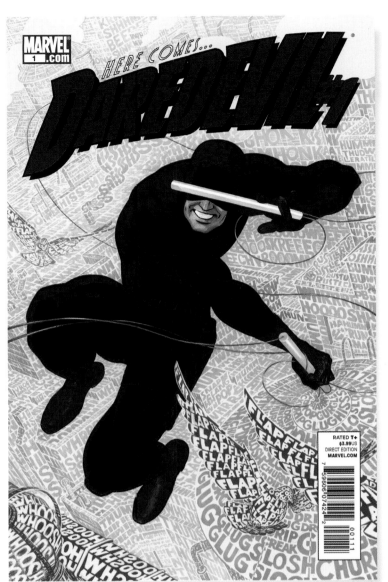

◄ *DAREDEVIL* #1

September 2011
Artist: Paolo Rivera

After years of dark stories, Daredevil's adventures took a new direction with this relaunch. Artist Paolo Rivera and writer Mark Waid brought back a sense of daring adventure to the Man Without Fear. Rivera's simple yet effective cover shows a smiling Daredevil in motion. The artist also found a clever new way of illustrating Daredevil's radar sense by surrounding the hero with words instead of images.

◄ *DAREDEVIL* #7

February 2012
Artist: Paolo Rivera

The image of Daredevil making a snow angel hints at the hero's near-death during an attempt to save a group of children caught in a snowstorm. Rivera's bold use of color—especially black and white—resulted in another eye-catching cover for one of the title's most critically acclaimed runs. The comic received a prestigious Eisner Award in 2012 for Best Single Issue.

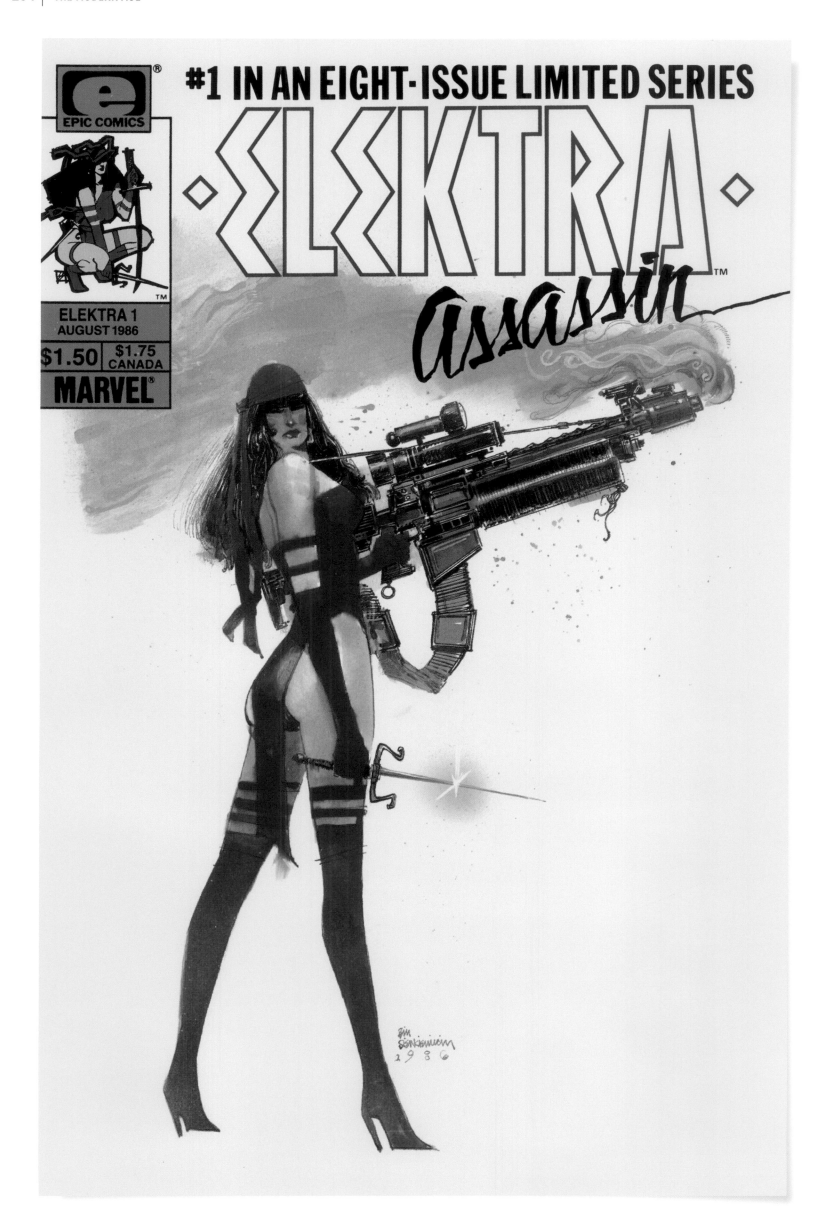

ELEKTRA #1 ▶

September 2001
Artist: Greg Horn

Elektra regained her own book in 2001 with Greg Horn providing many beautifully painted covers for the series. His artwork often featured Elektra in a combative pose—this first cover shows her wielding her deadly sai. Horn's realistic approach to the work added a layer of cold beauty to the complex character.

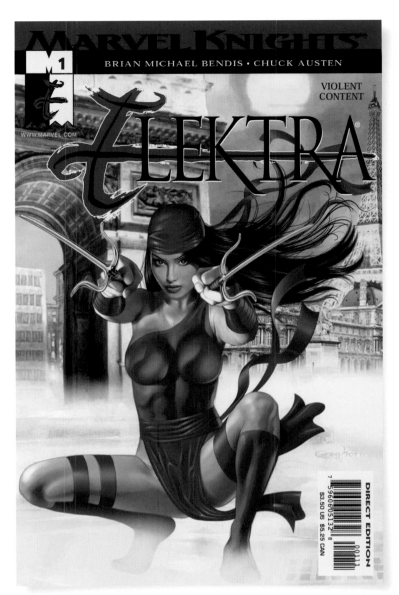

THUNDERBOLTS #1 ▶

February 2013
Artist: Julian Tedesco

Julian Tedesco was inspired by the look of the Thunderbolts' leader, the Red Hulk, on this eye-catching cover. The book saw the Red Hulk joining forces with some of Marvel's deadliest heroes—Elektra, Punisher, Venom, and Deadpool. The anti-heroes are tinted red on the covers to reflect the color of their leader, the Red Hulk.

◀ ELEKTRA: ASSASSIN #1

August 1986
Artist: Bill Sienkiewicz

The cover to the first issue of Elektra: Assassin saw artist Bill Sienkiewicz at the top of his game, creating a unique vision of the femme fatale and using a white background to give Elektra's red costume maximum impact. The series, written by Frank Miller, was published by Marvel's Epic imprint, which offered an outlet for more adult-oriented material, often featuring experimental visuals.

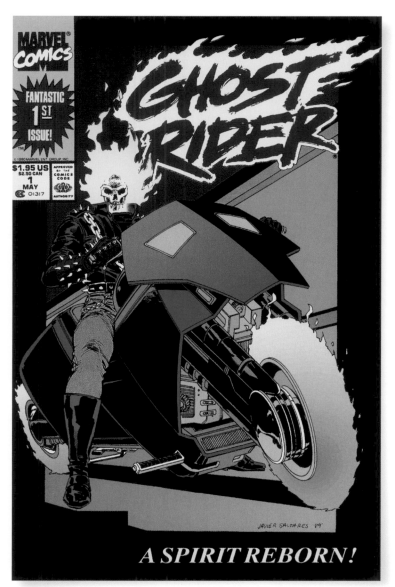

◄ *GHOST RIDER* #1

May 1990
Artist: Javier Saltares

A new Ghost Rider burst into action, as Javier Saltares revealed the new-look spirit of vengeance on the cover of the debut issue. The new title—featuring teenager Dan Ketch as the Ghost Rider— proved to be a smash hit, and it became one of the most popular Marvel comics of the time.

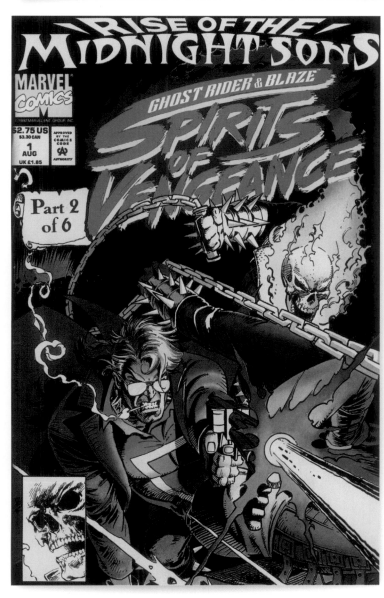

◄ *SPIRITS OF VENGEANCE* #1

August 1992
Artist: Adam Kubert

Adam Kubert's dramatic cover saw Johnny Blaze, the original Ghost Rider, team up with the latest incarnation. Kubert was a master of creating action scenes and dynamic movement, and he instills both characters with a sense of deadly energy in this cover portrayal.

◄ *GHOST RIDER 2099* #1

May 1994
Artist: Chris Bachalo

Ghost Rider 2099's first cover was an early work by Chris Bachalo, who created a new version of the Spirit of Vengeance, set in the far future. The frame around the main image is metallic ink, reflecting the cyberpunk nature of the new hero.

◄ *EARTH X* #1

April 1999
Artist: Alex Ross

Alex Ross' beautiful, painted art graced the cover of *Earth X*, a new series set in a dark future of the Marvel Universe. The cover for the debut issue showcases some of the strange alternate versions of the Marvel characters seen in the series, with the Earth X version of Captain America at the center.

▲ *PUNISHER #1*

August 2001
Artist: Tim Bradstreet

This Tim Bradstreet cover was the perfect piece of art to help launch a new series of Frank Castle's adventures. Skulls and guns were big recurring themes for the vigilante hero and both were present here, as an assassin put the Punisher in his sights.

▲ *PUNISHER #4*

May 2004
Artist: Tim Bradstreet

While most of Tim Bradstreet's covers focused solely on the Punisher, this chilling visual selected the terrifying moment Frank caught up with a victim. Bradstreet's realistic art brought a sense of grim emptiness to the Punisher, making the hero look more ruthless than ever.

◀ *PUNISHER #1*

March 2004
Artist: Tim Bradstreet

Writer Garth Ennis had reinvigorated Punisher as part of the Marvel Knights imprint. However, a big part of the revamped title's success was due to Tim Bradstreet's realistic covers. This artwork helped to launch a new run of the Punisher's adventures—under the banner of Marvel's Max Comics imprint, reserved for graphic content. The image of Frank Castle's armory was a chilling reminder of the hero's deadly war on crime.

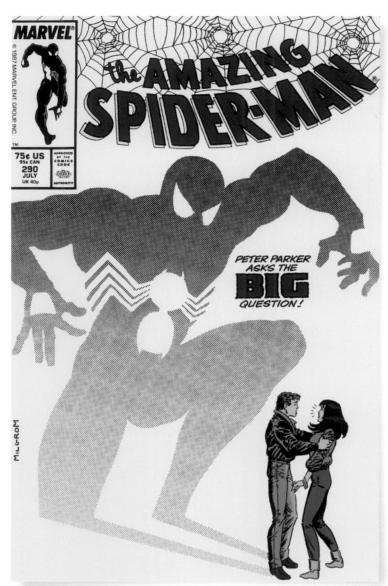

AMAZING SPIDER-MAN #294 ▶

November 1987
Artist: Mike Zeck

Kraven the Hunter looks his insane best on this cover for "Kraven's Last Hunt," regarded as one of Spider-Man's key stories. Artist Mike Zeck depicts the crazed state Kraven was in. His desire to prove himself superior to Spider-Man reached its shocking conclusion in this penultimate chapter.

◀ **AMAZING SPIDER-MAN #290**

July 1987
Artist: Al Milgrom

Al Milgrom's cover made pretty clear the big question Peter was going to ask inside. The use of white was perfect for focusing the attention on Peter and Mary Jane, reflecting the way a marriage proposal could make the rest of the world fade into insignificance. However, the shadow of Spidey looming over Peter and his bride-to-be adds a sinister edge to the piece.

◀ **AMAZING SPIDER-MAN ANNUAL #21**

1987
Artist: John Romita Sr.

It was the wedding of the year—Peter Parker and Mary Jane—and Marvel put their top artist, John Romita Sr., on art duty for the cover. Central to the image is the happy couple, but with Spidey's foes facing off against his allies in the background, it looked like the wedding might not go according to plan.

▲ *AMAZING SPIDER-MAN #312*

February 1989
Artist: Todd McFarlane

This Todd McFarlane cover features the Hobgoblin and the Green Goblin slugging it out with the webslinger caught in the middle. McFarlane's style makes the Green Goblin look crazier and more nightmarish than ever, while giving the fight scene a feeling of chaotic danger.

▲ *AMAZING SPIDER-MAN #313*

March 1989
Artist: Todd McFarlane

Todd McFarlane used his highly detailed technique to bring the Lizard to life on this cover. The close-up of the Lizard with its razor-sharp teeth, holding a seemingly beaten Spider-Man in his claws, creates a real sense of danger.

SPIDER-MAN #1 ▶

August 1990
Artist: Todd McFarlane

Following his huge success on *Amazing Spider-Man*, Marvel created a new Spidey title for Todd McFarlane to write and illustrate. McFarlane's debut cover illustration really adds the "spider" to Spider-Man, placing the hero in spider-like poses and adding intricate webbing detail. It became one of the most memorable modern-day images of Spider-Man and one of the biggest-selling Marvel comics of the decade.

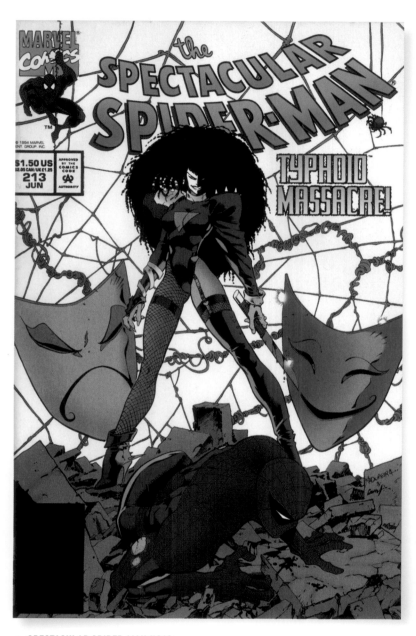

▲ *SPECTACULAR SPIDER-MAN #213*

June 1994
Artist: Joe Madureira

A young Joe Madureira produced truly stunning Typhoid Mary artwork for this issue. The frowning and smiling masks at either side of the villain reflect her split personality: On one side the deadly villain Typhoid Mary, on the other the mild-mannered Mary Walker. One of the villain's original creators, Ann Nocenti, was the writer on this issue.

▲ *AMAZING SPIDER-MAN #410*

April 1996
Artist: Mark Bagley

Carnage was one of the most popular Spider-Man villains of the 1990s, so when the alien symbiote possessed Spider-Man, the result was one of the most shocking covers of the year. Approaching the end of his five-and-a-half-year run on Spidey, Mark Bagley surpassed himself with an attention-grabbing fusion of the blood-red Carnage and a crazed-looking webslinger.

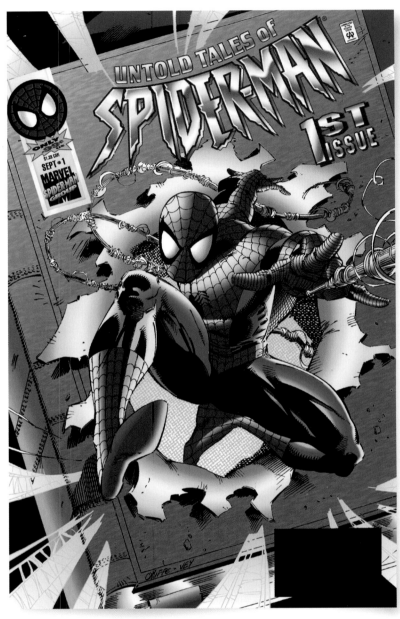

▲ *SPIDER-MAN #68*

May 1996
Artist: John Romita Jr.

The mid-1990s saw a lot of changes in
Spider-Man's comics. Many characters—
including the webslinger—were given
makeovers. This John Romita Jr. cover of
a new-look Hobgoblin debuted a more
menacing version of the villain, who now had
cybernetic modifications. The reflection of
Spidey in the pumpkin bomb is a nice touch, too.

▲ *UNTOLD TALES OF SPIDER-MAN #1*

September 1995
Artist: Pat Oliffe

Writer Kurt Busiek and artist Pat Oliffe
masterminded one of the most exciting
new Spidey titles of the decade. The cover
established what the new title was all
about: Spider-Man is shown bursting out
of an old book, revealing that this series
would tell new stories of Spidey, set during
his first few months as a hero.

▲ *PETER PARKER: SPIDER-MAN #75*

December 1996
Artist: John Romita Jr.

The "Clone Saga," one of the most controversial Spider-Man epics of all time, came to a shocking conclusion in this issue, with John Romita Jr. producing an action-packed wraparound cover. Fans had been split when Ben Reilly (Peter Parker's clone) had become Spider-Man, but this issue saw the old order restored. The cover revealed some of the dramatic changes within, as Peter Parker returned as Spider-Man to face the original Green Goblin—a villain he had thought was long dead.

AMAZING SPIDER-MAN #30 ▶

June 2001
Artist: J. Scott Campbell

J. Scott Campbell's striking image heralded the start of a bold new era for *Amazing Spider-Man* as shocking secrets of Spidey's origin were revealed. Writer J. Michael Straczynski and artist John Romita Jr. took over the title, with Campbell creating a number of stylish covers. As the hero learned that his powers were linked to an ancient spider-god, Campbell's artwork put the "spider" back into Spider-Man.

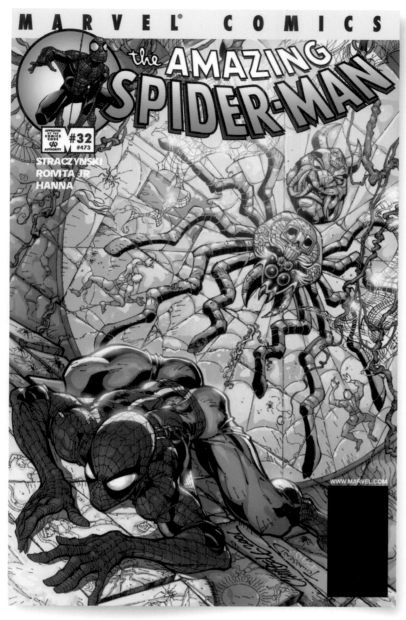

▲ *AMAZING SPIDER-MAN* #32

August 2001
Artist: J. Scott Campbell

J. Scott Campbell continued his run as cover artist on *Amazing Spider-Man* with another stunning piece. Campbell's cover hinted at the new, totemistic aspects of Spidey's origins that writer J. Michael Straczynski and artist John Romita Jr. were bringing to the title as they redefined Spidey's world.

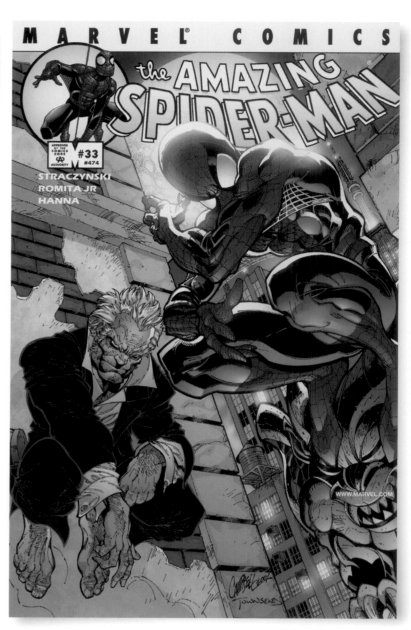

▲ *AMAZING SPIDER-MAN* #33

September 2001
Artist: J. Scott Campbell

Ezekiel, the man who had changed Spidey's life by telling him of his links to an ancient arachnid deity, appeared beside him on this cover. Campbell's depiction of Ezekiel looking like another, older "spider-man" was a sign that things were changing as one of the most original runs in the title's history continued.

AMAZING SPIDER-MAN #500 ▶

December 2003
Artist: J. Scott Campbell

Amazing Spider-Man went back to its original numbering for the 500th issue, with Campbell creating a truly dynamic cover featuring Spidey's most iconic enemies. The artist had burst onto the comic scene with his work for WildStorm, but his *Amazing Spider-Man* covers remain some of his best-known work. For this issue, he got to convey all the classic chaos and action that had made Spidey so popular.

▲ *MARVEL KNIGHTS SPIDER-MAN #1*

June 2004
Artist: Terry Dodson

With the stellar creative team of writer Mark Millar
and artist Terry Dodson at the helm, the launch of *Marvel
Knights Spider-Man* was bound to be something special.
Terry Dodson produced a wraparound cover for the first
issue, featuring Spidey and the Black Cat on the front with
four deadly foes pursuing them on the rear of the cover.
Dodson gave Spidey's enemies a spectacular menacing edge.

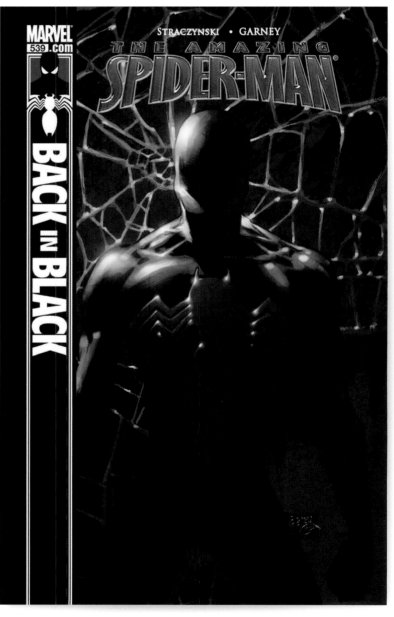

▲ *AMAZING SPIDER-MAN #529*

April 2006
Artist: Bryan Hitch

Spider-Man graced the cover of this issue in
a shiny, new armored costume. Created for
Spidey by Tony Stark, the suit would come to be
known as the Iron Spider costume. Meanwhile,
the strapline at the top also brings a sense of
foreboding as the Civil War—when Super Hero
would fight Super Hero—drew ever closer...

▲ *AMAZING SPIDER-MAN #539*

April 2007
Artist: Ron Garney

Following the events of the Civil War,
the world knew that Peter Parker was
Spider-Man. Aunt May had also been
shot, as Kingpin sought revenge on
anyone who knew Spider-Man. Garney's
cover image captures the webslinger's
dark and vengeful mood perfectly.

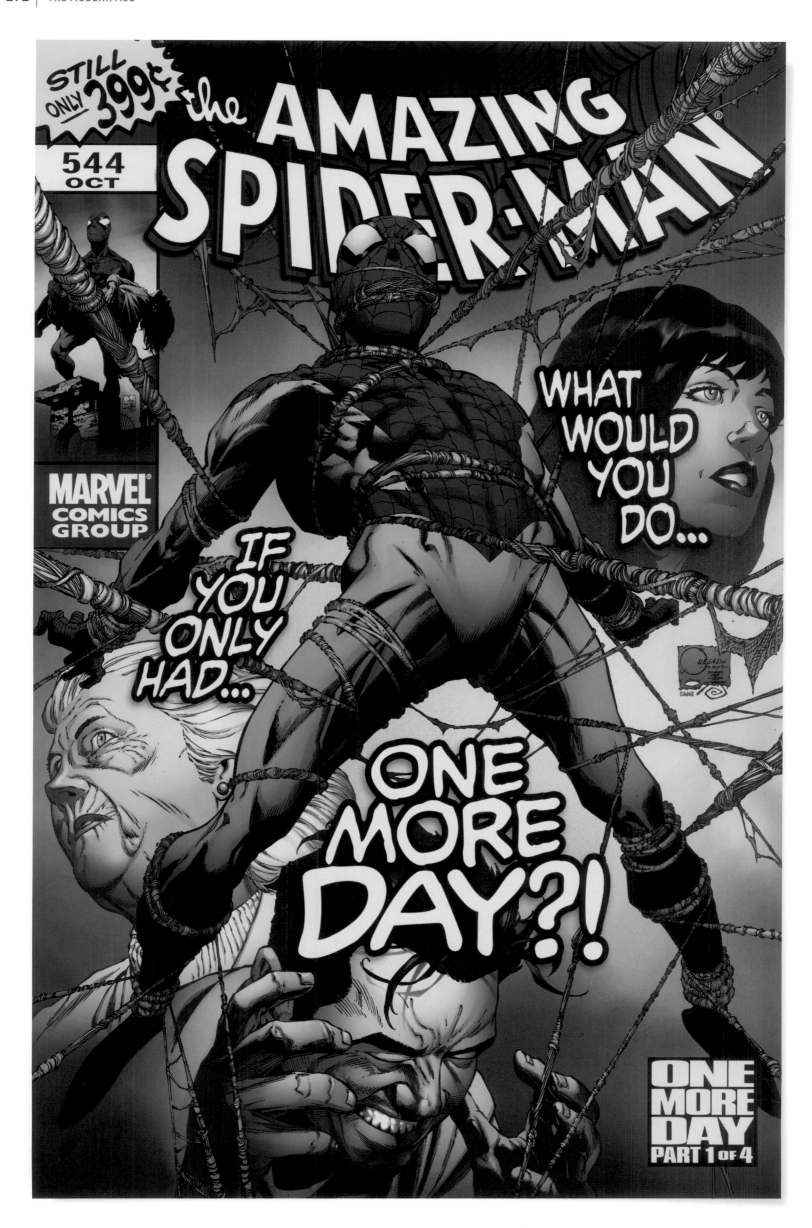

AMAZING SPIDER-MAN #560 ▶

July 2008
Artist: Marcos Martin

The experimentation with cover design continued with a fun layout by Marcos Martin. The background image has strong echoes of pop artist Roy Lichtenstein's work, and revealed a new villain: Piper Dali, a.k.a. Paper Doll. This mutant villain possessed the novel ability to make her body as thin as paper.

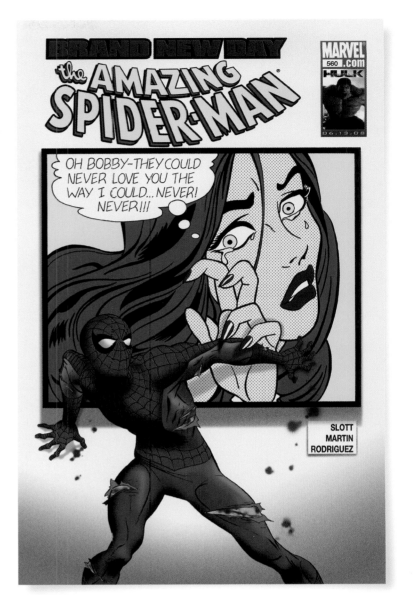

AMAZING SPIDER-MAN #561 ▶

August 2008
Artist: Marcos Martin

Paper Doll's eyes stare out at the reader from Marcos Martin's high-concept, collage-style cover, reflecting the villain's obsession with movie star Bobby Carr. The cover also hints at the idea of Mary Jane Watson (Bobby Carr's girlfriend in this story) being the Super Hero Jackpot, although this would later be revealed as a case of mistaken identity.

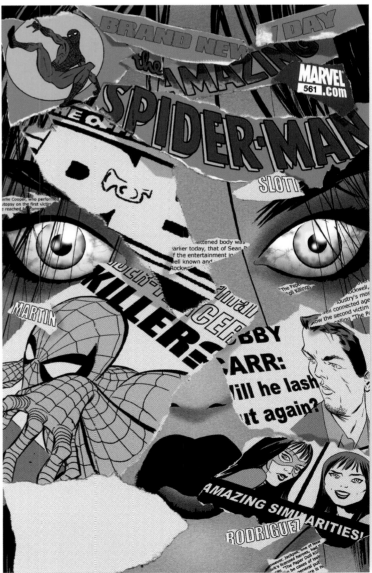

◀ *AMAZING SPIDER-MAN #544*

November 2007
Artist: Joe Quesada

"One More Day" was one of the most shocking storylines in Marvel's history as Spider-Man's marriage to Mary Jane was wiped out of existence. Quesada's powerful cover shows Spidey trapped by his own webbing—and torn between his love for Mary Jane and Aunt May. Spidey faced the hardest decision—to save Aunt May's life, he had to sacrifice his marriage to Mary Jane in a deal with Mephisto.

AMAZING SPIDER-MAN #555

June 2008
Artist: Chris Bachalo

It was, as the strapline stated, a
"Brand New Day" for Spider-Man,
whose adventures took an upward
swing following the events of
"One More Day." New villains and
characters appeared while artists
experimented with cover design.
Bachalo's image of Spidey and
Wolverine fighting Mayan
warriors, with only the heroes
in color, was an example of this
fresh and exciting new direction.

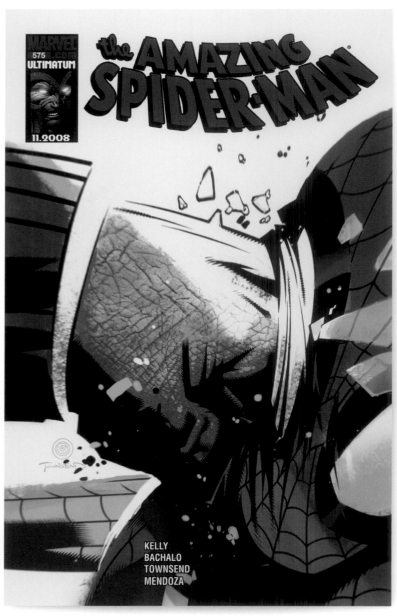

▲ *AMAZING SPIDER-MAN #568*

October 2008
Artist: John Romita Jr.

"The Brand New Day" era of Spider-Man saw Marvel experimenting with cover design, often employing interesting styles of typography, too. This cover, with "New Ways to Die" a prominent part of the artwork, reflected that trend. The dramatic image of Spidey revealing a Venom costume under his own clothes plays on a classic Super-Hero image, while the alien tendrils attacking the logo highlights the danger Venom represents.

▲ *AMAZING SPIDER-MAN #575*

December 2008
Artist: Chris Bachalo

It was a great time for artistic experimentation on *Amazing Spider-Man*, as this striking cover demonstrated. Bachalo's close-up of Spidey being punched in the face by Hammerhead is a strong image, especially with Bachalo's own, stark coloring work. The image has an even greater impact when seen in conjunction with the cover of the following issue.

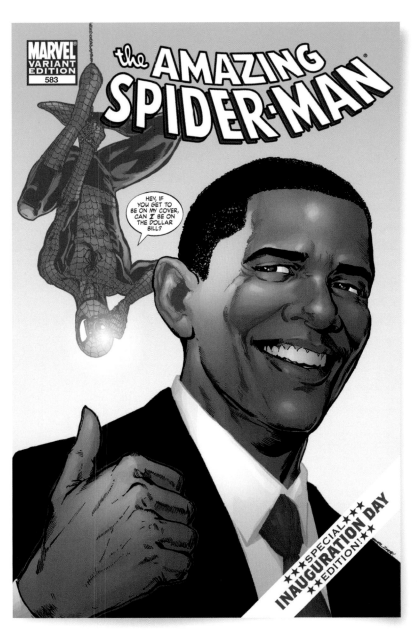

▲ *AMAZING SPIDER-MAN #576*

January 2009
Artist: Chris Bachalo

The second part of the Hammerhead story had the webslinger's response to the previous issue's cover—Spidey punched Hammerhead right back! Over the coming months, other linking themes would appear on the covers, but this black, white, and red two-image punch-up was one of the most dramatic—and amusing.

▲ *AMAZING SPIDER-MAN #583*

January 2009
Artist: Phil Jimenez

Every now and again a cover comes along that sums up the mood of a particular moment in time. This "Inauguration Day" variant cover did just that. Phil Jimenez put US President Barack Obama (a self-confessed comic fan) on the front of *Amazing Spider-Man* to commemorate his inauguration. President Obama also guest-starred inside the issue as Marvel celebrated a key moment in US history.

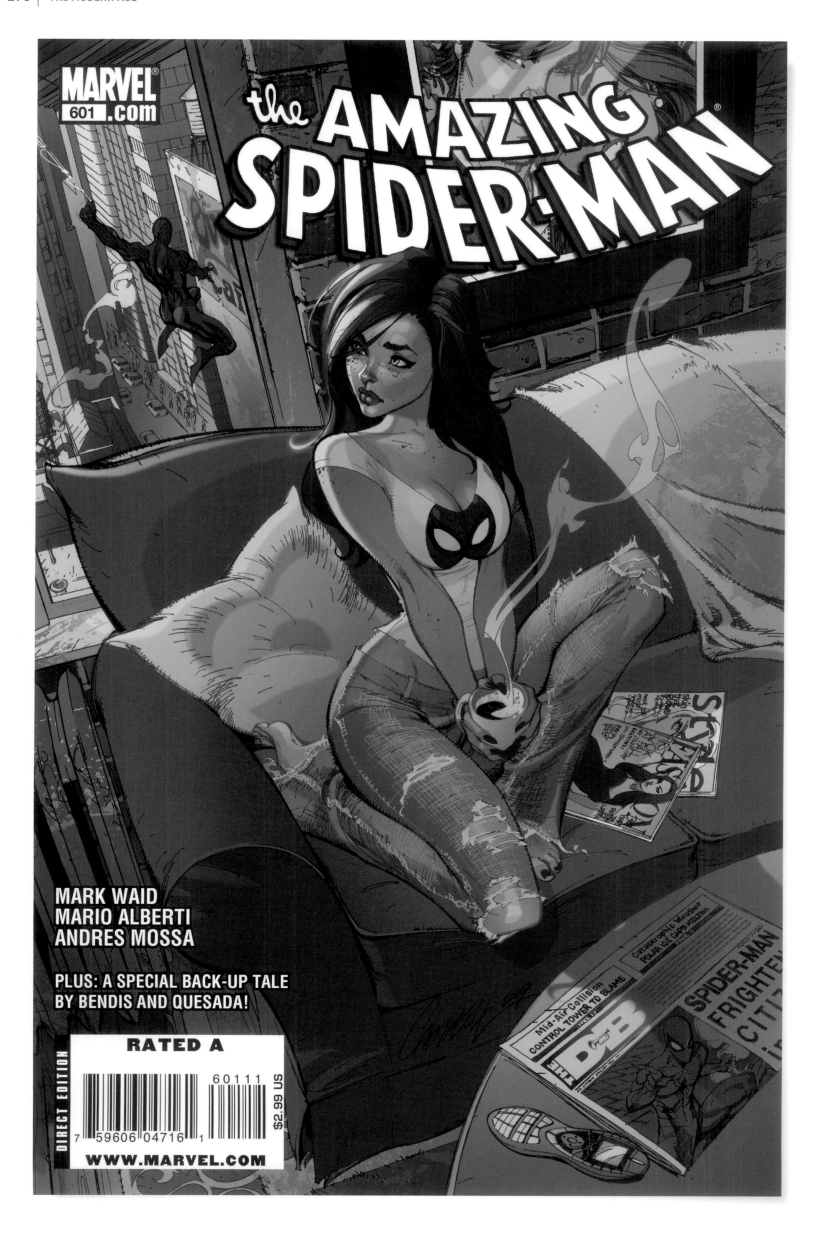

◀ *AMAZING SPIDER-MAN #601*

October 2009
Artist: J. Scott Campbell

J. Scott Campbell had always had a knack for drawing a great Mary Jane Watson, but this cover was something special. However, its appeal wasn't simply Campbell's winsomely pensive version of Spidey's ex. Readers were also thrilled by the inference that they were about to witness Peter and Mary Jane's first face-to-face meeting since "One More Day" had wiped their marriage from existence.

AMAZING SPIDER-MAN #607 ▶

November 2009
Artist: J. Scott Campbell

Spidey and the Black Cat teamed up again this issue. Campbell's alluring cover hints that Felicia Hardy (the Black Cat) hadn't quite given up her criminal ways or her obsessional love of Spider-Man. It also suggests that the hero and Spidey might be a little more than friends in this issue...

AMAZING SPIDER-MAN #619 ▶

March 2010
Artist: Marcos Martin

Marcos Martin proved himself to be one of the most inventive artists in the business with this striking cover. As red ink dripped from the slanted logo, it seemed that Spidey's life was about to take a deadly turn. But the story inside involved master of illusion Mysterio, so, of course, nothing was as it seemed.

▲ *AMAZING SPIDER-MAN #642–647*

September–November 2010
Artist: Marko Djurdjevic

The five-part "Origin of the Species" story saw Spider-Man
and a host of villains trying to find a baby that Lily Hollister
(aka Menace) had with Norman Osborn. There was a twist in the
tale too, when Norman's son, Harry, was revealed as the baby's
true father. This five-part series arc, and an epilogue to the end
of Spidey's "Brand New Day" era, featured six interconnected
covers by concept artist Marko Djurdjevic, showcasing the
numerous villains appearing in the story. The covers were
specially designed so they could be joined together to create
one enormous, action-packed image.

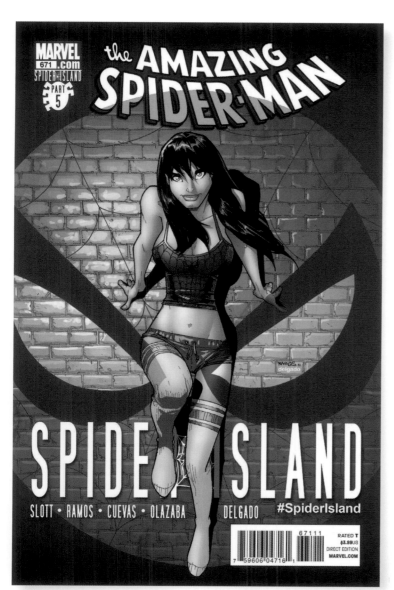

AMAZING SPIDER-MAN #700 ▶

February 2013
Artist: Mr Garcin

Marvel used this fantastic collage from Mr Garcin (an artist who specializes in collages made from Marvel comics) for what, at the time, was going to be the last-ever issue of *Amazing Spider-Man*. Garcin's work was the perfect choice for the final issue, honoring the changing styles of the wall-crawling hero since his debut in 1963.

◀ *AMAZING SPIDER-MAN #671*

December 2011
Artist: Humberto Ramos

The "Spider-Island" epic crossover saw the entire population of Manhattan gain Spidey-like powers before transforming into giant spiders, thanks to the machinations of the Jackal and the Queen. This cover focuses on a new role for Mary Jane in the saga as she temporarily gained spider powers to rival those of Peter Parker.

◀ *AMAZING SPIDER-MAN #678*

March 2012
Artist: Mike Del Mundo

Mike Del Mundo's cover makes it clear that something bad happened, as Spidey's battered hand reaches toward a *Daily Bugle* bearing the headline "New York Destroyed" and a strapline altered to read "The World's Worst Super Hero." In the time-travel story inside, Spidey was convinced that something was going to destroy New York in the next 24 hours, unless he could stop it.

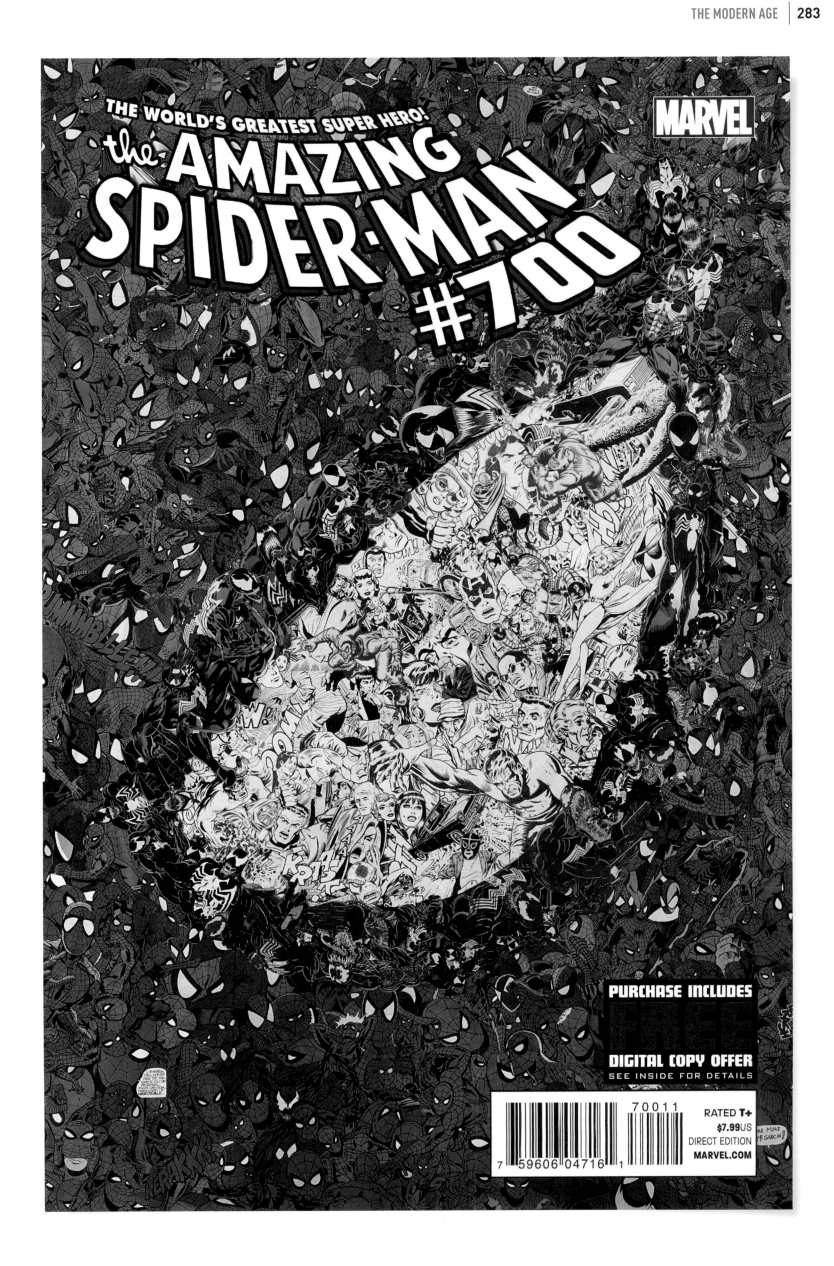

AMAZING SPIDER-MAN #1 ▶

June 2014
Artist: Alex Ross

Marvel released a number of variant covers to celebrate Peter Parker's return as Spider-Man. Alex Ross painted this masterpiece as a variant for issue #1—it was one of several covers he created that also celebrated Marvel's 75th anniversary. Ross' image was a celebration of Peter Parker as Spider-Man and features all of the most important things in Peter's life.

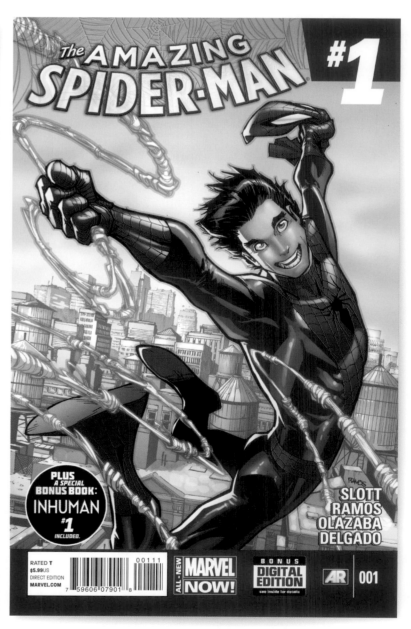

▲ *SUPERIOR SPIDER-MAN #1*

March 2013
Artist: Ryan Stegman

The old Peter Parker was dead—long live the new Peter Parker! With Doctor Octopus now masquerading as Peter, it was a time of great change for *Spider-Man* as *Superior* replaced *Amazing*. Ryan Stegman's cover showcases the new Doc Ock/Spidey as a different kind of webslinger, not just with a new costume but with a new superior—and deadly—attitude.

▲ *AMAZING SPIDER-MAN #1*

June 2014
Artist: Humberto Ramos

While it might appear as just a simple image of Spider-Man swinging through the city, the grin says it all—the real Peter Parker was back as Spider-Man. A whole new era of Spider-Man adventures was about to begin. It was one of the most upbeat Spidey covers in a long time.

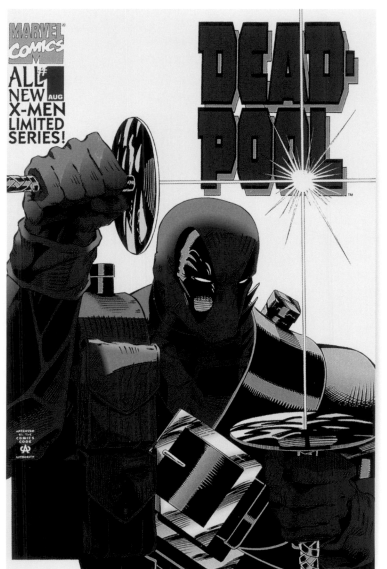

◄ DEADPOOL #1

August 1994
Artist: Ian Churchill

Ian Churchill illustrated the first cover to Deadpool's debut miniseries, focusing on a stylish body shot of the Merc with a Mouth. This early image is from a period when Deadpool was still more of an action star—albeit a slightly crazed one—in the style of Wolverine. In later years, Deadpool's style and stories would take a far more bizarre turn.

◄ DEADPOOL #11

December 1997
Artist: Pete Woods

By the time of his new ongoing series, Deadpool's adventures were starting to take a more humorous slant—as seen in this Pete Woods cover. The image is a homage to *Amazing Fantasy* issue #15 (August 1962; *see p50*), but it also reflects the story inside as Deadpool travels back in time to Spidey's early days. He even replaced the webslinger in an adventure that was a reworked version of *Amazing Spider-Man* issue #47 (April 1967).

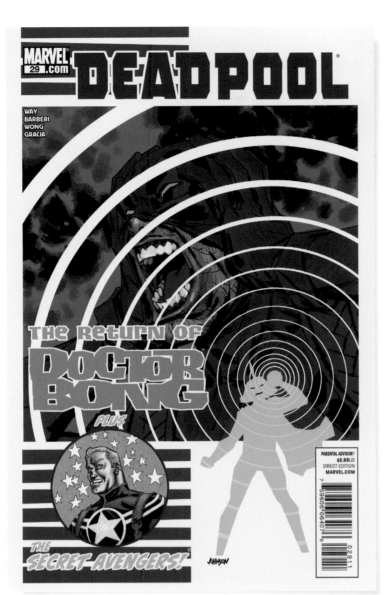

◄ *DEADPOOL* #29

January 2011
Artist: Dave Johnson

This issue harked back to *Howard the Duck* with the return of one of his old enemies, Doctor Bong. Dave Johnson's cover uses soundwaves emitting from Doctor Bong's helmet to maximum design effect. He also included a somewhat kitsch Steve Rogers' image, reflecting the way the title often satirized its stablemates.

◄ *DEADPOOL KILLUSTRATED* #1

March 2013
Artist: Mike Del Mundo

This cover followed Deadpool's shocking "realization" that he was just a fictional character and as such could never really die—unless he killed the literary archetypes of modern-day heroes and villains. Cue Deadpool literally hitting the classics. Each of the four issues took on the form of an old *Classics Illustrated* comics series cover (but humorously renaming them Deadpool "Killustrated"), starting with this *Moby Dick* homage.

X-MEN: PHOENIX—ENDSONG #1 ▶

March 2005
Artist: Greg Horn

Greg Horn cleverly portrayed Phoenix's deadly power in this image, as well as capturing the alien nature of the Phoenix Force. The red costume also indicates that this is the more deadly Dark Phoenix incarnation, while the flames behind reflect Phoenix's cycle of death and rebirth. A variant cover showed Phoenix in her original green costume.

◀ *ROGUE* #1

September 2004
Artist: Carlo Pagulayan

Carlo Pagulayan painted a number of beautiful covers for *Rogue's* third series, starting with this highly effective portrait. Pagulayan managed to capture not only Rogue's beauty, but also her aloofness and the alienation caused by her inability to touch anyone without harming them.

◀ *STORM* #1

April 2006
Artist: Mike Mayhew

Storm's second series focused on Ororo Munroe's relationship with the Black Panther. The headshots of Storm and the Black Panther above a romanticized heart-shaped tree and their younger selves suggest that this series would reveal the previously untold story of their first meeting.

▲ *WOLVERINE #24*

May 1990
Artist: Jim Lee

Few artists can be said to have defined
Wolverine as much as Jim Lee. While drawing
the X-Men's own adventures, Lee also
provided the occasional cover for Wolverine's
solo title. This neon-lit masterpiece showing
the hero in the far eastern island of Madripoor
was one such cover. Lee's Wolverine looks
truly deadly in this dark and dangerous image.

▲ *MARVEL COMICS PRESENTS #72*

March 1991
Artist: Barry Windsor-Smith

Barry Windsor-Smith provided covers
for each of the 12 chapters of his epic
"Weapon X" story, which was serialized
in the *Marvel Comics Presents* anthology.
This dramatic first cover hinted that the
saga would reveal one of the biggest
secrets from Wolverine's past—how he
gained his Adamantium skeleton.

▲ *MARVEL COMICS PRESENTS #84*

September 1991
Artist: Barry Windsor-Smith

The wraparound cover to the final chapter of the
"Weapon X" storyline features a close-up of Wolverine
with blood seeping from his Adamantium claws as
they pierce his own skin. Windsor-Smith's image
combines the wildness of Wolverine with a sense of
the character's humanity, while the story itself was
a big influence on the *Wolverine* and *X-Men* movies.

◄ *WOLVERINE* #35

January 1991
Artist: Marc Silvestri

Marc Silvestri illustrated one of the most critically acclaimed runs in *Wolverine*'s history and produced a number of action-packed covers during that time. This early Lady Deathstrike image is a prime example of Silvestri's dynamism and the gritty feel he brought to Wolverine's adventures.

◄ *WOLVERINE* #38

April 1991
Artist: Marc Silvestri

"Albert" was one of the more interesting additions to the Wolverine mythos. He started life as a simple android duplicate of Wolverine, programmed to kill the mutant, but soon became an interesting character in his own right. This dramatic cover depicts an early showdown between Wolverine and his duplicate.

◄ *WOLVERINE #43*

August 1991
Artist: Marc Silvestri

This atmospheric Marc Silvestri cover is all about color and texture. Here Silvestri used a rain effect and a strong red to create eye-catching artwork. The central pose reflects the story inside, with Wolverine seeking revenge on an insane killer who had tortured a wolverine in the Central Park Zoo.

◄ *WOLVERINE #77*

January 1994
Artist: Adam Kubert

Adam Kubert produced many outstanding images of Wolverine. This classic cover features the mutant suffering after Magneto had ripped the Adamantium from his body. The bandages around Logan's wrists, the result of his bone claws slicing through his skin with every trademark "snikt," added a new, painful dimension to the always troubled hero.

Adam Kubert's action scene of Wolverine and Gambit leaping from the rooftops is eye-catching enough, but the addition of overlaid sniper rifle sights gives the whole scene an extra sense of danger. Splitting the logo in two also cleverly helps to direct the reader's attention to the center of the action.

▲ *WOLVERINE #79*

March 1994
Artist: Adam Kubert

With its extended logo and shocking image of Wolverine in pain, clutching his broken claws, this classic cover shows a key moment in Wolverine's life. Kubert brought out the pain Wolverine was experiencing after his enemy Cyber snapped off three of his claws. Seeing the previously almost-indestructible Wolverine in agony was a big shock for long-term fans.

▲ *WOLVERINE #82*

June 1994
Artist: Adam Kubert

This relatively simple image was one of the most effective *Wolverine* covers that year. The stark black and white of the main image makes the blood on Wolverine's forehead and his yellow eyes even more striking. Moving the logo to the bottom of the cover was an innovative decision.

▲ *WOLVERINE #20*

December 2004
Artist: John Romita Jr.

John Romita Jr. was Marvel's leading artist when he teamed up with one of their biggest writers, Mark Millar, to create "Enemy of the State," a shocking story in which Wolverine is brainwashed by ninja assassins from the order known as the Hand. Romita Jr.'s wraparound cover portrays a bloodthirsty Wolverine after his run-in with the ninjas, who would soon brainwash the hero into being their deadliest member.

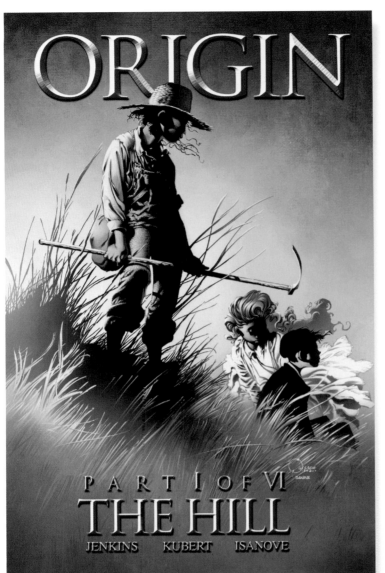

◄ *ORIGIN* #1

November 2001
Artist: Joe Quesada

It was the story that some thought would never be told—the origin of Wolverine. It was up to Marvel's then Editor-in-Chief and award-winning artist, Joe Quesada, to create something special for a story this big. His atmospheric cover, with the distinctive color work of artist Richard Isanove, is reflective of the story's 19th-century setting. Separate chapter headings on each of the four covers achieves a cinematic look.

◄ *WOLVERINE* #1

July 2003
Artist: Esad Ribic

Wolverine's third series went in a grittier and darker direction than the previous run. Esad Ribic's close-up of Logan might show Wolverine's claws, but it was a more everyday image of him than his usual costumed X-Men persona. The story inside was more "thriller" than "Super Hero," as Wolverine sought vengeance for a girl who was murdered after turning to him for help.

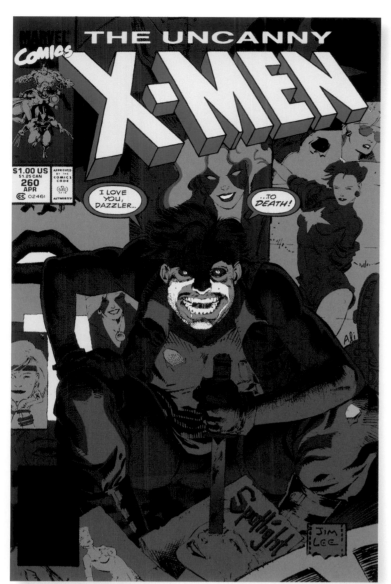

◄ UNCANNY X-MEN #260

April 1990
Artist: Jim Lee

Jim Lee reinvigorated the X-Men in the late 1980s. His sleek, action-packed style won him countless awards and he quickly became one of the most popular artists in the business. While Lee excelled at group shots of the X-Men, he could also produce atmospheric pieces such as this cover, showing a psychopath obsessed with Dazzler.

UNCANNY X-MEN #268 ►

September 1990
Artist: Jim Lee

Even by Jim Lee's high standards, this was a special cover—and a very special issue. The central image promised a team-up that comic book fans would love. This time it was Wolverine, Black Widow, and Captain America fighting alongside each other—and looking exceptionally heroic. The issue had a surprise in store too, as it was revealed that the three heroes had first met during World War II.

◄ UNCANNY X-MEN #269

October 1990
Artist: Jim Lee

Rogue and Ms. Marvel went way back. When Rogue was a villain, she accidentally stole Ms. Marvel's powers and memories. The two characters had met since, but this cover promised a much deadlier meeting. The image of Magneto's head at the bottom of the page, next to the words "Guess who wins!" suggested the meeting would have a surprise ending.

▲ *X-MEN #1*

October 1991
Artist: Jim Lee

Following the success of his work on *Uncanny X-Men*,
Jim Lee was at the helm for the launch of the first
new X-Men series since 1963. To celebrate this,
Lee created a huge fold-out cover for the first issue.
Each segment was released as a variant cover,
but another edition was released with all the
parts intact to fold out. The issue was a massive
success and became the bestselling comic of the year.

▲ *X-MEN CLASSIC* #57

March 1991
Artists: Mike Mignola and P. Craig Russell

This reprint of *Uncanny X-Men* issue #153
(January 1982) featured a beautiful new cover
by Mike Mignola and P. Craig Russell. The two
artists were masters of fantasy illustration and
the perfect choice for this issue, which was based
around a bedtime story Kitty Pryde told to the
young Ilyana Rasputin. While this reprint series
had started as *Classic X-Men,* it changed its title
to *X-Men Classic* from issue #46.

▲ *X-MEN CLASSIC* #63

September 1991
Artists: Mike Mignola and P. Craig Russell

Mike Mignola and P. Craig Russel. created
another masterpiece based on a classic
X-Men story—*Uncanny X-Men* issue #159
(July 1982)—where the team met Dracula,
who was attempting to make Storm his
vampire bride. Mignola and Russell's
work for these covers was so good, the
series was collectible for the covers alone.

◄ *CLASSIC X-MEN* #1

September 1986
Artist: Art Adams

Classic X-Men had a series of stunning covers
created by some of the best artists in the
business. Each issue reprinted an old X-Men
story, but also contained a second story by
John Bolton. The first issue's cover, by Art
Adams, was a celebration of the X-Men, with
all the mutants who appeared in the classic
Giant Size X-Men issue #1 (May 1975) brought
together in one stunning image.

▲ *X-MEN: ALPHA* #1

February 1995
Artist: Joe Madureira

The "Age of Apocalypse" was one of the *X-Men* comics'
biggest storylines. Set in a real ty in which Professor X
had been killed and had never formed the X-Men, it was
a massive multi-part epic the like of which had never
been seen before. Joe Madureira created an amazing
image of the alternate versions of the X-Men for the first
issue, *X-Men: Alpha*. The cover had shiny holofoil added
to the art to make it even more eye-catching.

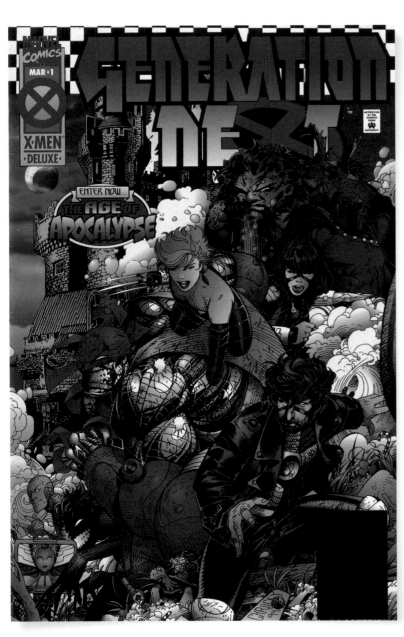

▲ *GENERATION NEXT* #1

March 1995
Artist: Chris Bachalo

All the X-line of comics were replaced by "Age of Apocalypse" versions during the event. Chris Bachalo was already producing wonderful art for *Generation X*, a new team of teen mutants, when he created this "Age of Apocalypse" cover for its replacement title *Generation Next*. The sight of the Generation X team in their Age of Apocalypse incarnations created an intriguing and memorable image.

▲ *WEAPON X* #1

March 1995
Artist: Adam Kubert

Perhaps the most shocking image from the early "Age of Apocalypse" covers was the sight of a one-handed Wolverine. The cover for the first issue of *Weapon X* had another shock for comic fans—the image of Jean Grey with Logan. In this dark reality the two were lovers, although events in the series soon forced them apart.

▲ *NEW X-MEN* #114

July 2001
Artist: Frank Quitely

It was all change for the X-Men in this issue as
writer Grant Morrison started his epic run on the title,
joined by artist Frank Quitely. The logo was redesigned
for the new era and the title renamed *New X-Men*.
Quitely's image of Cyclops and the X-Men moving
purposefully forward, dressed in their new paramilitary
uniforms, signified a real change in style for the heroes.

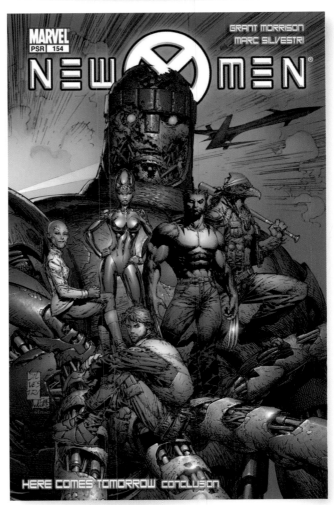

▲ *NEW X-MEN* #151—154

March 2004
Artist: Marc Silvestri

These four issues were an epic conclusion to Grant
Morrison's time as writer on *New X-Men*. Marc Silvestri,
one of the leading artists in the business at the time,
returned to Marvel for these issues and created a series of
stunning covers. The first three are futuristic incarnations
of Wolverine, Beast, and Nightcrawler, while the final shows
a dark, future version of Wolverine and his new X-Men team.

▲ *ASTONISHING X-MEN* #1

July 2004
Artist: John Cassaday

When artist John Cassaday joined forces with
movie writer-director Joss Whedon, the result
was one of the best X-Men comics of all time.
Cassaday created a number of stylish covers for
Astonishing X-Men, starting with this close-up of
Wolverine's claws, the light shining off the middle
claw providing an eye-catching flash.

▲ *ASTONISHING X-MEN #7*

January 2005
Artist: John Cassaday

Writer Joss Whedon made Cyclops one of his star
characters during his run on *Astonishing X-Men*, with
John Cassaday portraying Cyclops in a far more heroic
light than he had in the time leading up to the series.
This issue reflects Cyclops' resurgence under this team,
with Cassaday's cover showing the team seconds after
Cyclops' optic blasts had done their job.

GIANT-SIZE ASTONISHING X-MEN #1

July 2008
Artist: John Cassaday

Joss Whedon and John Cassaday's epic run came to an end with this heartbreaking special issue. Cassaday's wraparound cover shows the X-Men and their allies rushing into action to save Earth from the aliens of Breakworld. It was a battle not all of the team would return from.

▲ *UNCANNY X-MEN #448*

October 2004
Artist: Greg Land

Greg Land brought his realistic style to
Uncanny X-Men to create this moody close-up
of Wolverine. It was one of the few Wolverine
covers to keep the hero's face hidden. The concealed
features, coupled with the sight of Wolverine's
claws, add an element of mystery and danger.

▲ *UNCANNY X-MEN #449*

November 2004
Artist: Greg Land

Land produced a wonderful portrait of Storm for
this issue, showing Ororo Munroe embracing her
connection to the elements. Ororo Munroe had
always been a character who seemed happiest
in wide open spaces, and this cover reflects her
pleasure at being alone with the storm-ridden sky.

UNCANNY X-MEN #466 ▶

January 2006
Artist: Chris Bachalo

Rachel Summers, the daughter
of Jean Grey and Scott Summers from
the horrifying parallel Earth of "Days
of Future Past," was the focus of this
cover. Bachalo's use of flames around
both her and the logo is symbolic
of one of the books' deadliest stories,
as Shi'ar Death Commandos were
sent to Earth to execute every
member of the Grey family.

◀ *UNCANNY X-MEN #503*

December 2008
Artist: Greg Land

Cyclops' ex-wife Madelyne Pryor made a return in this issue. A clone of Jean Grey, Madelyne had turned into the Goblin Queen years before. The X-Men believed her to be dead, but Greg Land's cover hints at her return—and her role as the new Red Queen, the opposite of Emma Frost's old position as the Hellfire Club's White Queen.

◀ *UNCANNY X-MEN #504*

January 2008
Artist: Terry Dodson

This 1920s-style cover showcases Terry Dodson's attention to detail and skill in drawing female characters. Dodson's depiction of the female X-Men wearing unusual attire turned out to be because it was an image from Cypclops' mind, as his telepathic lover, Emma Frost, entered it to find out why he had been acting so strangely.

◀ *UNCANNY X-MEN #505*

February 2008
Artist: Terry Dodson

Despite the cover showing a group pose of the X-Men, this issue focused on the individual adventures of the team, rather than one big story. Dodson created a dramatic group shot, with the leader Cyclops in the forefront and the Blackbird aircraft taking off in the background.

◀ *UNCANNY X-MEN #535*

June 2011
Artist: Terry Dodson

A follow-up to Joss Whedon's *Astonishing X-Men* series sees Kitty Pryde as the focus on the cover. With the aliens from Breakworld returning, it was only natural that Kitty would be involved—in the previous series it seemed she had given her life to save Earth. The cover, which also shows the alien Ord and the S.W.O.R.D. space station, reflected the intergalactic scope of the new story.

◀ *UNCANNY X-FORCE* #1

December 2010
Artist: Esad Ribic

The first issue of the new *Uncanny X-Force* series saw Wolverine again leading a team of killers—"a Black Ops" version of the X-Men. The new series had the team trying to stop one of the X-Men's deadliest enemies— Apocalypse—from returning. Ribic's dynamic and moody art was a perfect fit for this new grouping, bringing out the deadly nature of X-Force in one tough group shot.

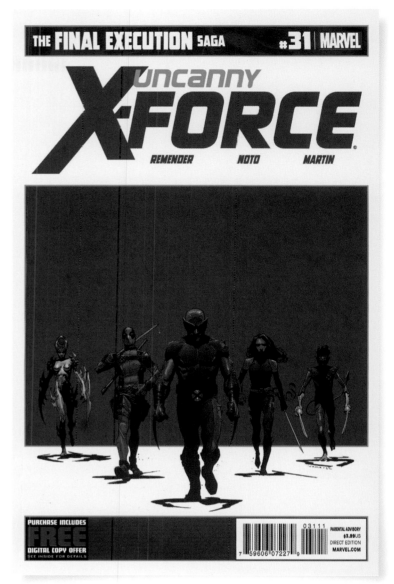

UNCANNY X-FORCE #31 ▶

November 2012
Artist: Jerome Opena

The "Final Execution" saga was the swan song for *Uncanny X-Force*. In this issue, Wolverine's son, Daken, formed a new Brotherhood of Evil Mutants to destroy the X-Force team. Jerome Opena's stylish two-tone cover reflects the dark nature and mood of the team as they prepared for their final battle with the Brotherhood.

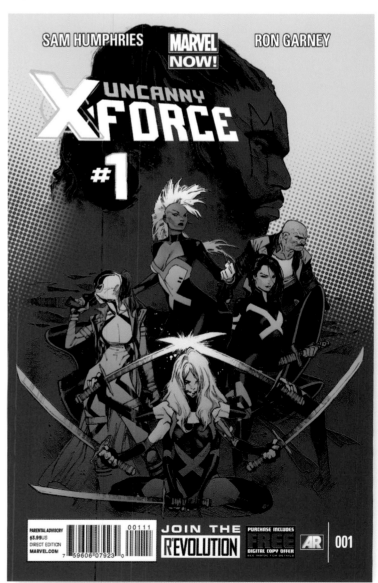

UNCANNY X-FORCE #1 ▶

March 2013
Artist: Olivier Coipel

A new X-Force team was introduced in this issue. Olivier Coipel's cover shows a group shot of the new team, which featured surprise members, such as the villain Spiral. It also promises the return of former X-Men member Bishop—shown looming in the background—without revealing whether he would return as a hero or a villain.

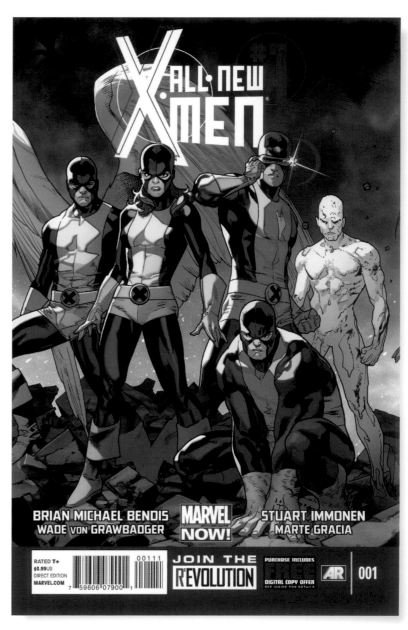

▲ *WOLVERINE AND THE X-MEN #3*

February 2012
Artist: Chris Bachalo

Wolverine and the X-Men quickly became a
favorite X-book for many fans. The stories
were set in the Jean Grey School for Higher
Learning, where Wolverine was headmaster.
Chris Bachalo provided a suitably surly image
of the popular Kid Omega (Quentin Quire) for
the cover, which captured Kid Omega's
rebellious attitude perfectly.

▲ *ALL-NEW X-MEN #1*

January 2013
Artist: Stuart Immonen

This new series reinvigorated the whole
mutant world by bringing the original five
X-Men through time into the present day.
Stuart Immonen portrayed the youth and
innocence of the young mutants on the
cover of the first issue, instantly intriguing
readers who wanted to see what would
happen when the young mutants met
their older selves.

▲ *UNCANNY X-MEN* #1

April 2013
Artist: Chris Bachalo

Bachalo's angled cover of the debut issue of a new *Uncanny X-Men* series reflects Cyclops' skewed view of the world—a world that now considered him a Super Villain. Cyclops' new visor was especially startling. The "X" represented the man Cyclops had killed while possessed by the Phoenix Force—his old mentor, Professor X.

▲ *X-MEN* #1

August 2013
Artist: Olivier Coipel

It was time for the women to take charge in the new *X-Men* series. While the *X-Men* comics had always included strong female characters, this was the first time they were featured in their own series. Coipel's eye-catching cover shows a dynamic group shot of the team, with Storm at the front, proving her leadership skills.

LONDON, NEW YORK, MUNICH,
MELBOURNE AND DELHI

Senior Editor Sadie Smith
Project Art Editor Owen Bennett
Edited by Jo Casey, Beth Davies, David Fentiman,
Gaurav Joshi, Tori Kosara, Catherine Saunders,
Chitra Subramanyam
Designed by Neha Ahuja, Karan Chaudhary
Senior Pre-Production Producer Jennifer Murray
Senior Producer Alex Bell
Managing Editor Laura Gilbert
Managing Art Editor Maxine Pedliham
Publishing Manager Julie Ferris
Art Director Lisa Lanzarini
Publishing Director Simon Beecroft

First published in Great Britain in 2014 by Dorling Kindersley Limited,
80 Strand, London WC2R 0RL
A Penguin Random House Company

10 9 8 7 6 5 4 3 2 1
002-195851-Oct/14

A CIP catalogue record for this book is available from the British Library

ISBN: 978-0-2411-8422-6

Printed and bound in China by Leo Paper Products

Discover more at
www.dk.com

ACKNOWLEDGEMENTS

Dorling Kindersley would like to thank: David Gabriel, Jeff Youngquist, Joseph Hochstein,
Mark Annunziato, Brian Overton, Sarah Brunstad and George Beliard at Marvel; Chelsea
Alon at Disney; Adi Granov for writing the foreword.

Alan Cowsill would like to thank: Nick Abadzis, James Britnell, Glenn Dakin, Aletia and
Gary Gilbert, James Hill, Adam Levine, Dan Rachael, Richard Starkings and Dean White
for answering the questions, and Matt McAllister, Maggie Calmels, Richard Jackson,
Ben Robinson, John Tomlinson, Colin Williams and the folk at Eaglemoss. Special thanks
to my Mum and Dad for buying me *Mighty World of Marvel* issue #1.